Life Is Like a Sailboat

Life Is Like a Sailboat

◠ Selected Writings ◡
on Life and Living
by John Grogan
for the *Philadelphia Inquirer*

Vanguard Press
A Member of the Perseus Books Group

Set in 12 point Bembo

Cataloging-in-Publication data for this book is available
from the Library of Congress.

ISBN 13: 978-159315-539-1

Vanguard Press books are available at special discounts for
bulk purchases in the U.S. by corporations, institutions, and
other organizations. For more information, please contact
the Special Markets Department at the Perseus Books
Group, 2300 Chestnut Street, Suite 200, Philadelphia, PA
19103, or call (800) 810-4145, ext. 5000, or e-mail
special.markets@perseusbooks.com.

10 9 8 7 6 5 4 3 2 1

Contents

Coming Home—and Moving On

The young woman waits just beyond the security checkpoint, craning her neck as disembarking passengers approach.

She is small and birdlike with short brown hair and a pretty, unadorned face that shows her emotions plain as a roadmap. She reminds me of a startled fawn, all senses on high alert.

I am waiting for a flight in the tiny airport in Columbus, Georgia, near the Alabama border. Columbus is home to the army's sprawling Fort Benning, a major deployment point for U.S. troops abroad. Soldiers are everywhere, coming and going. They stream through the security exit in their standard-issue camouflage.

The woman rises on tiptoes and looks past every one of them. Then she sees him, the soldier she has been waiting for. He spots her at almost the same instant and rushes forward.

He drops his duffel and pulls her into his arms. She surrenders without protest. They are blocking foot traffic. They do not care. They do not seem to even notice. They are lost in each other.

I wonder where he has arrived from—Iraq? Afghanistan?—and how long he has been gone. What is obvious is it has been too long.

A Silent Embrace

They hug silently for the longest time, rocking slightly on their feet, her face buried in his chest.

No words. None needed.

A full minute rolls by, and still they stand together in silent embrace. Finally, he pulls back and takes her face in his hands. And then they are kissing. Kissing like high school kids in the parking lot on prom night.

It is hard not to stare, not because of the scene's prurience but because of its beauty. A soldier has come home in one piece and this is his homecoming. In the age of the scripted media event, I have stumbled upon just the opposite: real Americans in the real America.

For most of us, America's warrior class remains comfortably out of sight. We go about our busy lives as the warriors fight and those who love them wait and worry.

We vaguely keep track of the bleak numbers—more than three thousand Americans killed, thousands more maimed and wounded, tens of thousands deployed halfway around the globe.

Yet it hardly seems real. Watching the couple, there is no denying reality.

As they kiss, the woman's shoulders begin to heave, and you can tell she is crying. Her soldier pulls back, wipes her cheeks with his hands and grins as if to say, "What are you crying for, silly girl? I'm home now."

He tosses his duffel over his shoulder and wraps his other arm around his girl. She leans against him, her towering oak. Through the glass doors, they disappear into the sunshine.

Welcome home, soldier.

A New Chapter

And now, a personal note.

Like that soldier stepping off the plane into another life, I'm stepping out of one role and into another. Today is my last as an *Inquirer* staff columnist. I am hanging up column writing to concentrate full time on book projects.

Publisher Brian Tierney and my editors want you to know that I was not a casualty of layoffs or cutbacks or any other fate. The decision was mine alone.

Those of you who have been following the last fifteen months of my life, in the wake of the surprise success of my book *Marley & Me*, know I've been trying to juggle essentially two full-time jobs, travel, and a family, not always very well. The bottom line: I am spread too thin.

There is another reason, albeit a secondary one: I love newspapers, especially this one. I believe in their value and future. But I don't know if I have the fortitude to stomach the dramatic cutbacks they are being forced to make in order to survive.

That's not to say I won't try to drop in occasionally with a guest commentary. I also invite you to visit my blog at www.marleyandme.com.

A writer without readers is not quite whole. You, *Inquirer* readers, have blessed me with the kind of audience every columnist covets: smart, opinionated, engaged. Right from the start, when I arrived here in 2002, you made me feel welcome. Many of you have come to be my friends.

Thank you for inviting me into your homes, your lives, and, on the best days, your hearts. It has been an honor.

Have a Litter-Less Little Christmas

I have good news for the Bag Lady of Roxborough. She is not alone.

Diane Bones is not really a bag lady. She is an employed, proud resident of the city's Roxborough section. But she is sometimes mistaken for a scavenger because of her habit of picking up trash along Ridge Avenue.

I called Bones a one-woman anti-litter campaign. I now know that's not the case. In the two weeks since I wrote about her, I have heard from dozens of like-minded eco-citizens who take it upon themselves to bend over and clean up after society's slovenly piggies.

They're fighting back one beer can, one cigarette pack, at a time.

I heard from Jonathan Haight of Downingtown, who reported: "As a member of a town-home community, I spend part of each week cleaning up around the court. Sometimes my neighbors laugh at me and call me crazy. I told one group of boys to pick up some chip bags they had dropped, and one just looked at me and said I was a 'litter-freak.'"

Jonathan, I hope you replied, "You're right, I am. Now pick it up before I rub your nose in it."

I heard from Joseph McCloskey, who wrote: "I am from Fox Chase, and I have been attending to the ritual of disposing litter during walks. I instruct my children that if you see trash, pick it up and take pride in your community."

Trash Attracts Trash

And from Alan Warren, who has been making daily litter pickups around his Chester County neighborhood since he retired eight years ago: "One of my motivations is the belief that trash attracts trash," he said.

There was Pauline Rosenberg from "Filthadelphia," as she heard a visitor call it, who wrote: "I do the same in Overbrook but with something called a 'grabber,' which you can get in a hardware store and allows you to pick up trash without bending over or dirtying your hands."

Judy Rubin can't pass by trash in her Mount Airy neighborhood without scooping it up. She commented: "Imagine the revenue the city would take in if it enforced the litter laws. I took a picture of a pole that had a sign, '$300 fine for littering.' Around the pole was trash a mile high!"

M. G. Phipps of Manayunk, frustrated by the city's refusal to replace a trash can that had disappeared from a neighborhood park, began tying a trash bag to the park fence, and changing it as needed.

Before moving recently, Allison McCool adopted four blocks around her home in the Fox Chase section of the city. "I wore thick gloves and wasn't afraid to pick up the broken glass or yucky items. I would keep going until my large trash bag was full. The local 7-Eleven allowed me to put the full bag into their bin."

Fighting Back

Boris Weinstein, seventy-five, of Pittsburgh, has dedicated much of his retirement to keeping forty blocks of his city litter-free. Weinstein began alone, and now has seventy volunteers scouring the streets daily. As he put it, "People who care must pick up for people who don't care."

Inspired by this army of do-gooders, I decided to give it a try.

As I headed out on a walk the other day, I spotted a plastic shopping bag in the weeds. Picked it up. Then began filling it. I scoured a stretch of road about the length of a football field. Here's what I nabbed:

Eleven beer cans, one vodka bottle, one whiskey bottle, a crushed Burger King cup, a Dunkin' Donuts cup, a McDonald's bag filled with packaging, two cigarette packs, a half-drunk bottle of Gatorade, various snack bags, loose paper. And most disgusting of all, a bottle filled with cigarette butts floating in an inch of fetid soda.

I recycled what I could, and threw out the rest. Part of me was repulsed, but a bigger part empowered.

And I thought: What if every person who reads this column joins the volunteer army? What if each one focuses on a single city block or the suburban equivalent? What if each takes ownership for keeping it trash-free?

Think of the difference we could make. Tens of thousands of blocks free of litter. We can do this. One person, one block, at a time.

The pigs will still be pigs, but the rest of us don't have to live with it.

Anyone care to join me?

Trash-Tossers Defile Our Region

Recently I was at Lake Nockamixon in upper Bucks County with my daughter, enjoying an unseasonably balmy day.

The last die-hard sailors were pulling out their boats for the season. A few fishermen cast lines. Hikers plied the trails. Couples sat on park benches. Children played.

It is a beautiful spot, with steep wooded hills rising from the water. Yet Colleen, who is nine, had an eye for only one thing—something I had learned to look right past.

"Dad," she said, crinkling her nose, "why do people throw their trash everywhere?"

Sure enough, the shoreline was littered with all sorts of flotsam from daily life—soda cans and juice boxes, cigarette packs and snack wrappers. Ten feet away sat a lonely trash can. I lifted the lid. It was empty.

How to explain this to a child? That some people consider the world their trash can? That they will drive for miles to enjoy the natural beauty of a place like this, and then think nothing of defiling it with their garbage?

How to explain that some among us don't give a damn about spoiling the experience for the next guy to come along?

That they assume there will always be someone else willing to clean up after them?

How to tell her that some people are, quite bluntly, pigs?

"I think some people just don't stop to think," I told her.

The Day's Good Deed

My daughter seemed to accept the explanation. Then, bless her little eco-heart, she began picking up trash and depositing it into the nearby can.

It was clear we weren't going anywhere until this chore was completed. I could wait or I could help. And so I joined her, and together we tiptoed over the boulders to reach every piece of junk we could find. Some of it clearly had washed up with the waves, and I tried to extend the benefit of the doubt: Maybe it had blown off boats, and the owners were unable to retrieve it. Some may have blown off picnic tables.

But a lot of the trash clearly had been dropped. Pigs, total pigs, I thought.

A half-hour later, the little peninsula we were on was clean. "We did our good deed today," Colleen said.

I suppose we had, but it was like spitting into a forest fire.

A few days later, she and I were walking down a country lane near our house. The road drops down a steep hill with dense woods and plunging ravines on either side. It is an idyllic stretch, the last place you would expect to find a de facto junkyard. But the roadsides were strewn with everything from whiskey bottles to bald tires to a rusty water heater. Drive-by dumpers had left whatever they no longer valued.

Near where a stream crosses beneath the road were signs of an underage beer party. Two dozen empty cans were left behind as a reminder.

Slobs Among Us

This time there was no picking up the mess. There was simply too much of it spread over too great a distance. A good project for a Boy Scout troop or youth group, I noted.

The next day I pulled into a public parking lot and found fast-food bags, drink cups, half-eaten sandwiches, and old newspapers left behind—all within sight of a waste can.

Trash, trash everywhere. Littering is a problem all over the world, but it seems to be a proud regional pastime here in the land of the Phillystines.

What gives?

I especially love the smokers who flick their smoldering butts out of moving cars as if they will magically disintegrate. Or even more, those who use their car ashtrays—then empty the whole ashtray in a parking lot.

Class act.

Take the litterbug challenge: Drive any stretch of roadway—city, country, suburban, it doesn't matter—and count how many items of trash you see. The results will astound you.

We have grown so numb to it, we look right past it. Sometimes it takes a child's eyes to see what we adults have learned to overlook.

We've turned this verdant, historic land of ours into a garbage dump.

In a world of seemingly insurmountable problems, this is one that is easy enough to solve.

Next time, throw it in the can, OK?

~~~~~~~~~~

Privilege of Class Has Limits on Main Line

On the Main Line, where money, class, and privilege collide
in a perfect storm of hyper-precious living, there are rules.
They are unspoken but ironclad nonetheless.

Poor Susan Tabas Tepper, the socialite who now finds herself in a bit of a legal jam, appears to have broken some real
doozies.

Roughing up the hired help at the mansion and then getting
trotted out in public for it is a mondo Main Line no-no. One
that can never be quite forgiven or forgotten at the country
club.

Très gauche!

Tepper, forty-three, lives in a sprawling, multimillion-dollar
estate in Villanova, a community if not at, certainly near, the
epicenter of the rarefied, Botox-and-liposuction Main Line
experience.

Lower Merion police in May arrested Tepper after her
housekeeper accused her of behaving very, very badly. It came
down to this: a messy refrigerator.

Domestic servant Xiomara Salinas told police she arrived at
work and was confronted by Tepper, angry about the refrigerator. Salinas said Tepper took out her displeasure by first
throwing a bag of carrots (gourmet organic, no doubt) at her,
then hitting her on the head with a telephone headset, pulling
her hair, breaking her eyeglasses, and trying to push her down
the stairs.

Temper, temper, my pampered little friend.

Relative Worth

Salinas told police that when she tried to flee, Tepper grabbed Salinas' purse and took $800, allegedly telling her: "You're not calling anyone. I'm important, you're nothing. No one will believe you."

You're nothing. Think about those words, and the hubris and disdain needed to hurl them at another human being. A human being who cleans up your messes because you can't be bothered.

I'm important, you're nothing.

Not exactly what you would hear Katharine Hepburn saying in *The Philadelphia Story*. Oh, dignified Main Line of yore, where art thou?

All of us are created equal. But we're not born equal. We don't grow up equal. We don't have access to equal education or opportunity.

Some of us are born into wealth, or marry or stumble into it. We park Range Rovers in our driveways, lunch the day away, and have more bathrooms than days in the week.

Others do what they must to survive. They leave their countries and risk everything to clean our toilets, rear our children, and pull our weeds. Often they work for low wages and without health care or other benefits.

The least the fortunate class can do is treat those who serve them with a shred of human dignity.

The least they can do is not throw carrots at them while telling them how little they matter.

Reversing Roles

Tepper, whom I was unable to reach by telephone Friday, remains charged with simple assault. Late last month she applied for a probation program in Montgomery County for first-time offenders. The program usually involves community service and allows defendants who stay out of trouble to ask to have their records expunged.

If the Villanova Volcano is convicted, I know just the perfect community service project for her—cleaning the homes of the service class. And cleaning them well.

Arriving early. Staying late. Returning home bone-tired after making other people's tile gleam. A few months on the other side of the Mop & Glo could do wonders for an attitude badly in need of adjustment.

But whatever happens in the criminal case is really not the point. Tepper's harsher sentence will come in the cool stares and whispered asides, the skipped invitations and subtle snubs of her peers.

She broke the rules. She will pay.

And unstated Main Line Rule #1 says that you don't embarrass yourself and your class by lowbrow displays of uppity contempt.

In the end, it all comes back to that simple rule we learned as children: Treat others as you would want them to treat you. No matter if you live in a mansion or ride a bus to clean that mansion, isn't that what it's all about?

In a word: Respect.

Amid the Beauty of Fall, a Brush with Mortality

The excursion was a mix of business and fall-colors sightseeing, a solo road trip that would take me as nearly as far as one can go and still be in Pennsylvania.

My destination was Warren, a lumber-and-oil town from another century nestled beside Allegheny National Forest in the northwest corner of the state, near the New York state line.

The drive out the previous day had been spectacular, the best October can give. The sun, perched in a cloudless sky, electrified the oranges and yellows and burnished reds that washed the mountains in watercolors.

Any time of year, Interstate 80 is one of the nation's prettiest stretches of pavement, climbing steep ridges and plunging through dramatic canyons. But in autumn, nature is on steroids.

I followed the interstate past Clearfield, then turned north on surface roads where the color show became even more bawdy.

The next day, my business behind me, I began the trip home in a steady rain. In the gray mist, the colors were muted but no less stunning. I settled into a comfortable pace, the drumbeat of raindrops on the car roof providing a staccato counterbeat to the steady slap of the windshield wipers.

In the downpour, my car felt like a cocoon, dry and safe. All was well.

A Sea of Red

Then came the brake lights. A few at first, followed by a torrent. Truck brakes bellowed; tires screeched. Traffic skidded to a standstill.

A few minutes passed and then, in my rearview mirror, I saw a parade of flashing emergency lights approaching: two ambulances, a police car, a fire truck. They raced past and stopped just up ahead.

As I crept forward on the right shoulder, the scene unfolded from the mist in vignettes.

The firefighters, many of them just kids, really, were jumping out of the trucks, popping flares. The paramedics pulled out their equipment. A trooper jogged to a jackknifed tractor-trailer. Off to my right, and down a deep ravine, I could see a passenger van.

The worst was still ahead. A second eighteen-wheeler had spun full circle, crashed through a guardrail, tipped, and slammed into a rock bank.

I did not envy the emergency workers whose job it was to make sense of the chaos and save lives.

As I inched my way through the wreckage, I marveled at how fast things fall apart. One moment, you are driving along enveloped in autumnal splendor. The next, your vehicle is plunging over a guardrail or heaving into an unyielding stone wall.

The utterly ordinary, in a heartbeat, can turn into the extraordinary. It can change life forever.

A Chain Reaction

Later, I would learn from Lawrence Township firefighters and the state police at Clearfield that the mayhem unfolded in two stages. One tractor-trailer lost control while braking. The second truck and the van skidded out of control trying to avoid the first crash. Two other truck rigs, I learned, then collided after I had passed through.

Miraculously, all injuries were minor, the fire department reported.

Just a few days after I passed through, however, another motorist was not so lucky. At almost the same spot, a jackknifed tractor-trailer led to a chain reaction in which an Ohio man burned to death after the car in which he was riding was rear-ended by a second truck rig.

It's human nature to pretend otherwise, but death can come anytime and anywhere. On a battlefield in Iraq or a playground in North Philadelphia; in an Amish schoolhouse or on a bucolic stretch of interstate surrounded by nature's most breathtaking palette.

As I cleared the crash scene and regained speed, I couldn't help but take a reckoning of life, in all its fragile, precious finiteness. Sometimes the world can seem like a shooting gallery, and we are the ducks.

I had merely been inconvenienced, but seconds earlier or later and who knows? A few days behind me, one less lucky would lie dead here, a victim of the random collusion of time and space.

I settled into the right lane and listened to the rain on the roof, the thump of the wiper blades.

Life was short. Impossibly beautiful. Wildly unpredictable. Worth embracing every moment of every day.

***

Pack Them Off, but Never Forget

Vikram Dewan leads the way down a sun-dappled path at the Philadelphia Zoo, where he recently took over as president and chief executive officer.

He is eager to point out the many innovations and improvements for the nation's oldest zoo.

The renovated big-cats exhibit reopened in May with more cats, more up-close viewing opportunities, and a whiz-bang interactive learning station for kids.

Plans are advancing for a bigger and better children's petting zoo, slated to open in 2009, replacing the antiquated one that has been in place for nearly half a century.

A $6 million makeover of the birdhouse is on the drawing board.

Dewan, a compact man who sports wire-rimmed glasses and a beatific smile, wants to trumpet the zoo's bright future. He leads me through gaggles of happy youngsters and moms with strollers.

But before we have walked fifty paces, the one topic Dewan would just as soon not talk about is literally staring us in the face.

Up ahead are three of the zoo's four elephants, standing close together in their small, dusty enclosure, looking lugubriously out over the crowds.

The elephants are magnificent creatures, and on this day, as on most, they draw some of the biggest crowds.

An Undeniable Sadness

Yet there is something undeniably sad about them, these intelligent and complicated mammals hardwired to roam freely across the vast savannas of Africa penned into a mere one-third of an acre.

It's a little like squeezing four humans into a phone booth and saying, "Have a happy life."

Because the three African elephants don't get along with the sole Asian elephant in the tight confines, they are kept segregated.

The zoo has had elephants since it opened in 1874, but their captivity in such tight quarters has become a source of mounting protests and bad PR in recent years.

Dewan arrived in July to inherit a raging controversy: Was it possible to keep such social, free-roaming creatures in the tight confines of an urban zoo totaling just forty-two acres?

In the end, Dewan and the zoo's board answered no.

By deciding earlier this month to donate the animals to larger facilities, they basically agreed with protesters that the animals deserve better. "It's absolutely the right answer for where we are today," Dewan says. "Always the welfare of the animals came first."

The zoo was unable to raise the $22 million needed to expand the elephant quarters, and even if it had, the biggest space available would have been a couple of acres—still woefully insufficient.

"We're bounded on all sides," he says. "At best it would have been a temporary solution—three to five years—and a very expensive one."

Starting Over

And so in the spring, the three African elephants—Petal, Kallie, and Bette—will take a road trip down Interstate 95 to six-acre digs at the Maryland Zoo in Baltimore. And the lone Asian elephant, Dulary, will be alone no more, enjoying life among her own kind on an open 2,700-acre sanctuary in Tennessee.

It's the right thing to do.

Every zoo lover no doubt will miss the sagacious elephants so central to the experience. And the financially struggling zoo's gate numbers could suffer without their drawing power.

But keeping them would have come at too great a cost—not so much financial as moral.

Zoos exist not only to amuse and entertain but to teach and instill understanding of, and respect for, other species and their habitats. The whole concept is slightly incongruous. Can we really expect to imbue children with respect for other species by pulling the animals from their native habitats and imprisoning them behind bars?

Yet it is the elephants that are most emblematic of this disconnect.

If the Philadelphia Zoo really wants to teach visitors about the elephant's wild majesty and special place in the animal kingdom, here's an idea:

Build an exhibit explaining the long history of these amazing animals in captivity and why the nation's first zoo will no longer be a party to it.

A Searing Lesson in Forgiveness

In hindsight, I realize I was driving too fast, especially given the rain-slicked roads.

Ahead of me at an intersection, a car was stopped with its left blinker on. I bore down, expecting it to turn out of my path at any second.

But the car did not turn. By the time I hit the brakes it was too late. I skidded and slammed into its rear end, catapulting it into cross traffic.

Miraculously, the other vehicles all avoided the car, but I realized instantly my moment of poor judgment could easily have resulted in the death of an innocent stranger.

Across the intersection, we both pulled into a parking lot. The man inside looked like he could have been a bar bouncer, large and intimidating.

He wasn't hurt and neither was I. His car did not even have a dent where I had hit it.

"Man, you almost got me creamed," the driver said.

I apologized profusely. He had every right to be angry, and I was braced for him to get in my face, poke a finger in my chest, and dress me down with a string of obscenities. People had been beaten up, even shot, over lesser transgressions.

Then he did an amazing thing. The stranger shook my hand and said, "It was an accident. Don't worry about it."

The F-Word

That was years ago, but the moment has stuck with me because it put me on the receiving end of an important lesson. I had erred and he had forgiven.

Forgiveness.

We all want to think we are capable of it. And for most of us, most of the time, we are.

We can forgive a child who disobeys. Or a delivery driver who accidentally knocks over our mailbox. Perhaps even a thief who takes what is ours.

But what about an offense far worse? Unspeakably, unimaginably worse?

What about a stranger who barges into a country schoolhouse, lines up ten innocent children against the chalkboard—and opens fire?

What parent, what community, could forgive that?

We now know the answer.

Within hours of Charles Carl Roberts IV's murderous assault on the Amish school in Lancaster County on October 2, the local Amish community was already expressing forgiveness.

Even before they had a chance to bury their dead daughters. Even as they huddled bedside as other victims clung to life by the most tenuous of threads. Complete and total forgiveness.

What was done was done, and the killer, too, was now dead. No amount of anger or vengeance-seeking would bring the children back or the killer to justice. The Amish had two choices: Descend the dark staircase into bitterness, or follow the tenets of their faith and rise above it. They believe that all acts, even one as monstrous as this, are part of their God's inexplicable plan.

And so they forgave.

Mercy Amid Grief

Amish neighbors went to the killer's home to console his wife and other relatives. They attended his funeral, and invited his widow to attend at least one of the murdered girls' funerals. As thousands of dollars poured in from around the world to help the families of the victims, the Amish set up a fund for the killer's own children.

Unbelievable.

Unbelievable and somehow beautiful all at once.

It is the stuff sermons are built around. If the Amish can forgive such a ghastly violation, can't we all try to be just a little more forgiving of the slights and hurts and wrongs of daily life?

The simple people know what many of us still have not figured out, that the ever-escalating violence of vengeance has no end, and that the acid of revenge etches the human heart with deep and permanent scars.

Imagine if the ethic of unilateral forgiveness could envelope the Sunnis and Shiites in Iraq, the Catholics and Protestants in Ireland, the Jews and Palestinians in Israel. Imagine if it could permeate the streets of America, where rival gangs kill over colors and young men settle scores over respect with 9 mm Glocks.

The Amish have found the road to a higher place. The rest of us could do worse than to be a little more like them.

September Light Darkens Morning

If April is the cruelest month, as T. S. Eliot so famously proclaimed, then September surely should be the kindest.

The heat and humidity of August are gone, swept away by dry, crisp air that carries the faint promise, but none of the gloom, of the autumn to come. Sunset, that impossibly late-night showstopper of summer, returns to a more civilized hour. The goldenrod has turned the meadows to yellow.

The days are mild, the nights perfect for sleeping beneath an open window, a blanket pulled to the chin.

The light is different this time of year, radiant and slanted and full of hope. A light you'd expect to find in Tuscany, yet here it is on a sleepy hillside in Pennsylvania, shafting through the white pines, bathing the towering cornfields in gauzy gold, dancing over the soybeans. A happy light.

A happy light, and yet this is the very same light of that morning five years ago today. The light of that brilliant and dreadful day.

The light through which we all watched loaded jetliners crash into filled office towers. The light through which television cameras captured innocents plunging to their deaths.

September 11, 2001. Is it possible that half a decade already has passed?

We have come so far and moved so little. Our troops have chased terrorists into the most remote corners of the planet. Our country has marched into a war that no one, not even the president, can quite explain.

At home, we Americans sit zombie-like as our civil liberties quietly erode. We swallow hard and shrug off the concept that the United States of America, this great, big-hearted land of freedom and liberty, might be condoning torture.

It's a different age, a different time, we say with resignation. Sadly it is. In many ways our lives have returned to normal. Once again, we are free to follow the ups and downs of Brad and Angelina and Jen and Vince. We listen in as cable television obsesses about the disappearances of pretty white girls.

And just when life seems utterly mundane again, we find ourselves standing in long security lines dumping our shampoo and toothpaste into trash bins, wondering whether the next passenger's soft drink might be an explosive in disguise.

I walked through my garden the other morning, the dew still heavy in the grass, and checked the pumpkins ripening in the sun. I sampled a still-tart apple off the tree and examined the pears swelling toward perfection.

Then I looked at my watch: 8:45. The pure, blue skies of September brought it all back again.

The first plane was bearing down on the North Tower right at this minute on that gin-clear morning five years ago, I noted. In sixty more seconds everything would change forever, but in this minute America ticked on like clockwork. The second plane was seventeen minutes behind.

United Flight 93, which would come down in a western Pennsylvania meadow amid a passenger revolt against the terrorists in the cockpit, had taken off from Newark.

Another routine September morning just like this one.

There I stood amid nature's steady assurances. Amid all these lovely reminders of life's reliability. Reminders that the seasons turn to years and the years to decades, that the fawns grow to bucks and the delicate maple buds of spring become the riotous palette of fall. Reminders that life's cycles continue without noticing the machinations of man.

And yet.

September, this gentle, sweet month, will never be the same.

The heart's surge cannot help being tinged with sadness. You see that light, that amazing, luminous light. You smell the earth's fecundity, take in its beautiful rhythm. And it all comes back.

That day. You know where you were, and I know where I was. We always will.

The gentle season forever will hold this now—a generation's greatest sorrow. The two have become one. At least in this lifetime, the crisp, clear skies of September will stand as an annual reminder of, and the most eloquent memorial to, that day.

As the sun warms my face and the bees stagger like drunks on their overload of nectar, I want to believe it is nature's way of whispering to each of us on this fifth anniversary that goodness and gentleness will someday prevail.

~~~~~~

A Big Gust, a Pivotal Moment

That summer's day would mark the end of an era—the last time my father and I set sail.

Dad had brought home the *Wayfarer* when I was ten, and for the next fourteen years the graceful little sailboat with the mahogany seats would play a central, defining role in the Grogan family summers.

Each Sunday, we'd be out there on the lake, Dad and his three sons, scooting over the water on journeys to nowhere.

My father had grown up a landlocked city kid, much of it in the Germantown section of Philadelphia, and had learned to swim only when he joined the navy, and then not well. He wanted more for his kids.

He and my mother saved and moved us out of the city to a neighborhood on Cass Lake in a suburb of Detroit. Unlike either of our parents, my siblings and I grew up as comfortable in and on water as sea otters.

For Dad, sailing was a mysterious challenge outside his comfort zone. He read books, studied charts, enrolled in classes. For his youngest son, it was second nature. I took to it like youngsters take to a second language, effortlessly and intuitively.

By the time I was in high school and at ease sailing solo or with friends, Dad began to make excuses for staying ashore. Gradually, I figured out that he had spent all those Sundays on the water not so much because he loved it but because he wanted his children to.

I went away to college and then took a newspaper job in a small town on Lake Michigan. Each summer I faithfully returned home to put the boat in the water, where it mostly would sit at its dock unused.

That's where it was on a late-August weekend in 1981 when I came home to visit and invited Dad to join me for a sail.

"You go ahead," he said.

"Come on," I coaxed. "For old time's sake."

Dad relented and off we went. I was at the helm, a stiff breeze filling the sails, whitecaps breaking over the bow. After a while, I handed the tiller to my father. He hadn't sailed much for years, and I could see he was a little unsure of himself.

But soon the old spark seemed to return, and I saw a smile on his face as he gazed up at the wind vane. All was well.

Then the big gust came.

It slammed into us and buried the boat's rail under water. I let the jib fly to dump its wind and scrambled to the high side.

My father, like every sailor, knew the remedy for a strong gust: Luff the sails and point the boat into the wind. On this day, he froze.

"John! Take it!" he cried, and his voice had an edge I did not recognize.

Dad was always the cool, collected one. When there was a crisis or emergency, he was at his best. Calm, in charge, taking control.

My whole life, he had been the strong oak to my spindly sapling, the one I always turned to for strength and security. I grew up confident he could right any wrong, fix any problem.

Now in an instant, a wall of water pouring into the cockpit, our roles were reversed.

"John! Help!"

I lunged for the tiller, but was too late. The boat flipped up on its side and swamped.

Dad was a retiree now with a heart attack under his belt. I knew he was getting on in years but I had never quite accepted that the oak in my life would ever be anything but.

In that moment, I felt fiercely protective of him.

"It's OK, Dad. We're OK," I said.

I helped him up onto the overturned hull and got him into a life jacket.

"Just sit tight," I said, then swam another life jacket out to the tip of the mast so it would not sink.

By the time I swam back, The Oak was back, calm again, acting a little sheepish about his momentary freeze and flash of panic.

"We're fine," I said, grinning. "We'll have this baby up in no time." And we did. In all our years sailing together, it was the first time either of us had capsized. It was also the first time my father had called on me in a moment of crisis to help him.

As we limped back to shore, I teased him gently about breaking our perfect, fourteen-year record. But inside, I knew this would be his last time in the *Wayfarer*. I knew our family sailing days, those magical shared moments that had cemented a son to his father, were done.

Even in the instant, without benefit of reflection, I under-stood the significance of the day. It was the watershed moment in which our paths—mine rising into adulthood, his on the long, slow descent toward life's conclusion—had crossed.

It was my turn to start looking out for him now.

"Quite a day," Dad said when we were back on land.

"Quite a day," I agreed.

<hr />

Time Powerless to Heal This Hurt

To a mother who has lost a son, ten years is really just a heart-beat. A single, blinding moment in space and time as intense as a muzzle flash.

Friends and neighbors move on. Relatives move on. The police move on.

A mother cannot move on.

This is Yvonne Reyes' reality.

One instant she is telling her teenage boy to eat a good breakfast; the next she is staring at his locked-in-time photo-graph, realizing a decade has passed since she last kissed his cheek or brushed the hair from his eyes.

"He will always be seventeen," she said.

November 18, 1996, was just another ordinary Monday. Reyes, a graphic artist, was working at her studio in Hunting-don Valley. At 3:30 P.M., the telephone rang. The younger of her two sons, Gabriel Hanemann—born on Mothers Day 1979—had been rushed to Albert Einstein Medical Center with a bullet in his chest.

"On the way to the hospital, I'm doing the 'Please God, please God, don't let him be dead,'" Reyes remembered recently.

God did not hear. At 3:42 P.M., before she could even arrive at his side, Gabriel was pronounced dead.

Like that, it was over. The child she had carried in her womb, nursed, nurtured, and raised to the brink of adulthood, was gone.

Hanemann had driven with two of his classmates from William Tennent High in Warminster to the Olney section of the city. The mother still is not sure why.

Shot Through the Heart

What she knows is this: Her son was at the wheel, idling in the parking lot of a doughnut shop when an armed assailant rushed the car in an apparent robbery attempt. When Gabriel refused to unlock the door, the man, described as eighteen or nineteen, fired one shot through the window and into Gabriel's heart.

The teen put the car in park, got out, and staggered a few feet before collapsing. The killer fled, never to be apprehended. The death merited brief mentions in the *Philadelphia Inquirer* and *Daily News,* and nothing more.

Gabriel was just another anonymous victim of gun violence in the city, one of the hundreds who fill the morgues and news briefs columns each year.

For several weeks, the police stayed in touch with the mother. But with no new leads to report, the calls became increasingly uncomfortable. "The detective finally said to me, 'You have to move on,'" Reyes said.

As if that were an option.

Sitting in her sun-dappled studio, whimsical silk butterflies dancing in the window, she said, "I just don't believe in closure. What is that?"

She picked up a framed photo of Gabriel. Slender and handsome, he is playing bass guitar on stage with his high school rock band. "A very sweet boy," she said, tears returning once again. "Very sweet."

If gun violence is an American epidemic, too vast and numbing to fully absorb, an afternoon with this still-grieving mother is a reminder that behind every black-and-white homicide statistic is a flesh-and-blood human being—and a family left behind.

Channeling Grief

Not that Reyes is spending her life moping. She continues to run her own graphic design shop in Huntingdon Valley and is proud of and close to her remaining son, Matthew, thirty.

She has tried to channel her grief and anger into constructive channels.

She supports gun-control advocacy groups and in 2000 participated in the Million Mom March on Washington to protest gun violence, an event she found oddly empowering. All around her at the rally were other mothers, just like her, who had lost children to guns. Who understood.

Over time, the grief once so palpable on her face has moved inside her, invisible to casual observers. She soldiers on with life. As she puts it, "I get out of bed every morning."

That is as much as she can ask for.

Ten years later, the unsolved murder gathers dust in the cold-cases file. Gabriel's classmates are having children of their own now, some named in honor of the slain teen. Fresh killings fill the newspapers. The world has moved on—except for one.

The mother cannot. Not this decade, not next.

She misses her son. What she would give for one more hour with him.

New Jersey Beaches Not Land of the Free

I was sitting on the beach in Avalon last week, white sand between my toes, salt breeze in my face, a giant yellow sun perched perfectly in an endless blue sky.

The day was about as perfect as beach days get. So why was I feeling so grumpy? I should have been daydreaming about fanciful pursuits or simply staring happily out to sea.

Instead I fretted about American core values and what strikes me as a gross violation, at least in spirit, of one of the most basic of them all.

No, I wasn't thinking about unconstitutional detentions at Guantanamo or secret wiretaps of Americans or tortured rationalizations for torture.

I was thinking about something much closer to home—or, as the case was on this day, much closer to my oceanfront hotel.

Yes, I was stewing about that oh-so-un-American of government impositions: the dreaded, evil beach tag.

My wife, our daughter, and I had arrived at our hotel before check-in and had decided to kill time until our room was ready with a walk in the surf.

But when we tried to walk over the dune onto the beach, we were greeted with a reminder that this little corner of the land of the free requires a paid pass for entry.

No problem. The hotel had provided two tags with our room, but still it reminded me of the one thing I hate about the Jersey Shore—the brazenly undemocratic, exclusionary practice of charging Americans for access to a public American treasure.

A Sovereign Right?

Does anyone own the sand? Does anyone own the surf? Does anyone own the sunshine or the shells or the lonely cries of a soaring gull? So why do we line up like sheep to pay for the privilege of enjoying what no man, no government, can possess?

Maybe my dark mood was the result of growing up on the Great Lakes surrounded by hundreds of miles of pristine, white-sand beaches that anyone could enjoy anytime. No fees, no badges, no police-state grumpy guards manning the dune line. (Is it me or are all beach-tag checkers suffering some degree of Napoleon complex, little people overcompensating in a big way?)

Maybe it's because I spent a dozen years living near the ocean in South Florida, where beach communities without exception manage to maintain clean, safe, fun beaches without onerous access fees.

Maybe it's because I had just returned from Santa Barbara, California, where stunningly beautiful beaches were open and free to all.

My friends who grew up going to the Jersey Shore each summer shrug their shoulders and look at me like I need a Valium refill. "It's five bucks a day," they say. "What's the big deal?"

No big deal for them or for me or for most of us. But as I sit on the beach, my tag pinned securely to my swim trunks so I don't raise the ire of the Little Corporals prowling about, I think about the ranks of low-paid workers, many immigrants, who keep beach towns like Avalon humming.

A Shared Treasure

I think about the maids who change the beds and the gardeners who trim the hedges and the busboys who clear the dirty plates. What about them?

They work all week so the rest of us can play. On their day off, shouldn't they have the right to bring their children to the beach, too, without having to shell out the better part of an hour's pay per family member?

It's not the money; it's the principle. What next? Pay-as-you-go public drinking fountains? A fee to breathe fresh air?

I know what the beach towns say: that keeping clean, safe, lifeguarded beaches costs money, and the burden should be placed on those who use them.

But what would Walt Whitman say? What would Thoreau say? And Jefferson and Adams and Franklin?

What would Woody Guthrie, the balladeer who wrote "This Land Is Your Land," say? Would he have sung, "This land was made for you and me (and anyone else who can afford the fees)"?

Yeah, I'm a little grumpy. Maybe it's the heat. Maybe it's because I wasn't ready to say goodbye to the Shore.

Maybe it's the fact that a beach tag should fit any self-respecting American about as comfortably as a tight swimming suit filled with wet sand.

Obeying the Law at Personal Peril

I've pulled a lot of dumb stunts in my life, but this one was arguably the dumbest of them all.

It was nuts. Crazy. Reckless and death-defying. I planned to drive on the Philadelphia-area highway system—going the speed limit.

Ridiculously foolhardy, I know.

My mission was to drive to work with my cruise control set exactly on the posted limit and not a mile per hour more.

Yes, I know. Only the exceptionally foolish and the truly suicidal drive the speed limit on Philly-area highways where pedal-to-the-metal, cell phone–distracted, lane-weaving, passive-aggressive drivers are legendary. It is an invitation to be steam-rolled, rear-ended, squashed like a little bug.

My inspiration for this exercise in civil obedience came from a veteran area educator who had become so dismayed by the aggressive driving on the Pennsylvania Turnpike he decided to document the number of cars and trucks that blew past him as he obeyed the law.

Harry Finlayson lives in North Wales, Montgomery County, and commutes every day to New Jersey, where he is a guidance counselor in the North Hanover School District.

Finlayson is a fastidious, by-the-rules kind of guy who believes that if everyone stayed near the posted limit, a lot fewer people would get hurt and killed in crashes each year.

A Close Call

Last month, Finlayson was driving east on the turnpike near the Fort Washington exit at his customary 68 m.p.h. in a 65 m.p.h. zone when a large semi-tractor-trailer came right up on his rear end in the middle lane and stayed there, just three feet off his bumper, finally passing him on the right. The truck then cut him off—on purpose, Finlayson believes. He called the episode "a near-death experience."

That got the educator upset enough to document the realities of turnpike driving. Using a clicker, he logged every car he passed and every car that passed him on his daily commute during the month of May. The results are not exactly a news flash.

On average during the month, 273 cars per day blew past him as he went the speed limit, while he passed only an average of 3.6 vehicles, most of them heavily loaded trucks struggling up grades. Along the way, he got a lot of dirty looks and tailgating from drivers who didn't appreciate him slowing down the daily Philly 500 white-knuckle commuter race.

"In short," he said, "I am being punished by other motorists for driving the speed limit, especially by truckers."

You sure are, Harry. There's nothing worse than a law-abiding citizen mucking up our roadway anarchy.

A Forty-Mile Experiment

I decided to try my own experiment, beginning at the Quakertown exit on the turnpike's Northeast Extension and continuing to the Route 3 exit of the Blue Route in Delaware County, and then back north to the Schuylkill Expressway, a total of about forty miles.

As I started out on the toll road, I set my cruise control exactly at 65 m.p.h. Almost immediately, other cars began to whiz by.

Business people in imports, construction workers in pickup trucks, landscape crews hauling trailers, grandparents in boat-like Buicks, moms in minivans with infant car seats in back. They all passed me as though I were the tortoise and they the hares.

A big rig rode my tail for a mile, its grill filling my rearview mirror, before it, too, rumbled past me.

After the Mid-County toll plaza, the speed limit dropped to 55 m.p.h.—and I adjusted my speed accordingly. This made only one difference: the speed at which my fellow commuters blew past me. The lower speed limit did not appear to dampen their accelerator enthusiasm one bit.

One guy in a pickup truck shot me an exasperated look as if to say, "What's your problem, pal?"

My problem was that I was following a speed limit that had no grounding in the reality on the road. I felt like I had a scarlet S-for-slowpoke emblazoned across my hood.

By the time I had concluded my experiment, 238 vehicles had raced by me in a blur. Vehicles of every shape, size, model, and description.

How many did I pass? Exactly zero.

Debate Over Ring Engages Readers

I'm not the only one who has plenty to say about The Ring.

Readers have been peppering me with their opinions on the guy who gave his girl a very large engagement diamond, then changed his mind and asked for it back. Classy.

As the story, first told by the *Inquirer*'s Mario F. Cattabiani on Valentine's Day, unfolded, Janet Grace said forget it; Mario Mele said see you in court.

Why settle for premarital sex when you can have premarital depositions?

The jilted bride-to-be had donated the princess-cut gem to charity (that'll teach him!), and the turncoat groom demanded that she pay him the full value plus $100,000 for his headaches.

After their acrimonious engagement became the talk of the town, they settled quietly, agreeing to keep the terms undisclosed.

Others have not been so reticent.

So I don't get anyone in trouble with spouses, ex-spouses or thankfully-not-quite spouses, we'll keep today's discussion on a strictly first-name basis.

Take it away, Shellie from Wynnewood: "Despite what the law says, human decency says otherwise. If the woman ends it, give the ring back. If the man ends it, suck it up."

John from Holland landed squarely on the woman's side, too: "Calling off the engagement should be considered a breach of contract, and such an action forfeits any claim to the ring."

Think Long and Hard

James from Doylestown offered this advice: "The best thing for men to do is to think hard before you decide to marry the woman of your dreams. Once you make the choice and once you propose to her, then she is yours for posterity. . . . "

A grandmother named Edith did not mince words: "Was he that stupid to think he could stab his fiancée in the heart and get his ring back?"

Marc threw a whole new wrench into the works: "I agree with you 100 percent about letting the scorned bride-to-be keep the engagement ring. But, suppose it's something of personal value, like your dog. Would you give him up without a fight? I don't think so. I wouldn't."

He then asked an interesting question: "Say your dog's barking to come in at the back door. Your wife, who lost her keys, is yelling at the front door to come in. Who do you let in?"

Marc, I refuse to answer on the grounds I may be banished to the couch.

Others shared their own stories.

From Michele: "I was once engaged, and I received my ring on my twenty-first birthday. Tooooooo young. I realized that I was making one of the biggest mistakes of my life, and I called off the whole thing. It was one of the hardest things I have ever done. I gave my ring back. I didn't want anything to remind me of him. That is why I don't understand why she wanted to keep the ring."

Calling All Cupids

Another woman told this story: "Back in 1990, my fiancé, whom I loved dearly, broke our engagement two weeks before the wedding in a most unceremonious manner—and asked for the ring back. I took the ring off my finger and handed it to him. Later that week, when I went to pick up my things at his home, he had already packed them in boxes, and on the kitchen table was a check for $1,000, which I left behind. Now, sixteen years later, your words only confirm what I know about this man."

She signed her letter: "Never Married, But Not Sorry."

Guys, take a hint here: If you're going to dump a woman, don't try to pay her. Just a little tacky.

Finally, there was this from Lloyd, who is still licking his shattered-engagement wounds: "It is a two-way street, pal. I was engaged once. We told each other about our love and devotion and lifelong commitment to each other and it was true to the heart. At least it was for me."

Uh-oh. I don't like where this is going.

"I found out a few months into the engagement, as we were working on plans for the ceremony and reception, that she had a male 'friend' on the side. Yes, you better believe I deserved that ring back. It wasn't a gift. It was a sign of commitment on both our parts. Mine by giving and hers by accepting. She reneged." Ouch.

Lloyd, meet Never Married. Never Married, say hello to Lloyd. Life is short; hope springs eternal.

A Run of Cowards on Region's Roads

One was a homeless man on a dark street.

One was a twelve-year-old girl who darted off the curb while playing.

One was a nun walking to morning Mass.

One was a fifteen-year-old girl talking on her cell phone, and one a fourteen-year-old boy heading to a 7-Eleven.

One was a tow-truck driver who had stopped to help a stranded motorist.

Some lived in the city, some in the suburbs. They came from all walks of life.

All had one thing in common: They were killed by hit-and-run drivers.

Hit and run. The term does not quite do justice to the act. In the hierarchy of illegal behavior, there are more heinous crimes, but surely none more cowardly. To take a life, by accident or recklessness, or some combination of the two, and then to simply run away and leave a dying person in the street—well, it takes a special breed of human to do that.

Some of these deaths might have been merely accidents, not crimes at all, had the driver only had the decency to stop. Some might have been deemed the fault of the pedestrian. But a motorist becomes a felon the moment he chooses to run.

Slight Hesitation

The most recent victim of the region's open season on pedestrians, Sister Paul Mercedes Perreca, was fatally struck near dawn Monday as she walked from her parents' home in the city's Mayfair section to attend 6:30 A.M. Mass. The driver of the Ford pickup truck, police said, hesitated before speeding off.

During that hesitation, I imagine, a brief moral dilemma played out. Shock, then recognition followed by panic. A once-in-a-lifetime moment—the choice between moral courage and reptilian expediency. The driver knew the right thing to do, then pushed the gas pedal.

Just four days earlier, Royale Harris, twelve, was struck in West Philadelphia after she darted into the street. She likely would have survived had the driver only stopped instead of leaving her lying in the path of traffic, where a second car fatally hit her.

And before Royale, there was Ashlee Mohacsi, fifteen, killed as she walked along a traffic lane in Burlington County on New Year's Eve, talking on her cell phone.

And before Ashlee, there was Anna Almond, fifty-two, struck by a car as she walked to a friend's house in Camden. She died several days later.

And before Almond was Rasheen Newkirk, fourteen, a Bensalem High freshman who walked with a limp, struck and killed as he made his way across Street Road. The next day, police arrested an illegal immigrant who they say had been driving without a license.

Too Many to Name

And before Rasheen, there were many, many more—too many to recount here. All with one thing in common: a driver without the moral barometer to stop and take responsibility.

Some of the deaths drew big headlines and community outrage, such as that of fifteen-year-old Kayla Peter, struck down last summer as she walked home in Northwest Philadelphia by a white Lexus that fled. A former Queen Village restaurateur, who a grand jury found was highly intoxicated that night, awaits trial.

Some were barely noticed, such as the hit-and-run death of Robert Janaitis, thirty-one, a tow-truck driver from South Philly killed by a Mercedes-Benz as he helped a motorist on Interstate 95. It took five weeks—but police made an arrest.

Then there was the most sensational of them all—the hit-and-run death of the homeless veteran in Harrisburg that eventually sent a former state representative, Thomas Druce of Bucks County, to prison.

It comes down to this. Each of us someday, perhaps when we least expect it, will face that watershed moment that will define all others in a life. The moment that puts our humanity to the test. For some it will come on the battlefield, for others in a hospital room, or workplace, or marriage. For still others, it will come behind the wheel of a car on a dark night with a stranger's body suddenly . . . just there.

When that moment arrives, we each need to ask ourselves: Which path will it be?

⌒

You've Got Spam: AOL's Trial CDs

As I hauled the fifth bulging bag of trash to the curb after the holidays, I knew I had finally had enough.

The packaging that comes with nearly every purchase in this country, be it fast food or appliances or underwear, is totally out of hand. Do we really need that pint-size action figure double-boxed and shrink-wrapped and bound to a cardboard slab with nylon straps? Are we worried he'll escape?

Do we think those zucchini will somehow taste better sold on a foam tray and wrapped in enough cellophane to cover the Wachovia Center?

I had recycled as much paper and plastic as I could, and still my family of five was contributing mounds to the landfill—most of it useless packaging that came into our house with gifts and immediately went into the trash. It was obscene.

That's when I spotted the enemy. In the top of an open trash can, waiting to join the parade of flotsam on the curb, sat two unopened, plastic-wrapped boxes that had appeared in my mailbox days earlier like so many uninvited packages before them.

If an old flame were mailing me unwanted items, I'd be filing a stalker complaint with the local police. But these weren't from an old flame.

They were from America Online.

One was addressed to me by name, the other to "Current Resident." Both contained identical materials: shiny new CDs and an offer to "Try AOL 90 days risk-free!"

An Uninvited Guest

The only problem was I didn't want to try AOL, risk-free or not. I'd been there, done that, and moved on to another Internet service provider years earlier. And yet, with the regularity of rainfall, the unwanted CDs showered in. As soon as they arrived, I would drop them in the trash.

Maybe it was the postholiday grumpies, but I said out loud, "Not this time." I pulled the two AOL boxes out of the trash and scrawled in bold letters across them: "Refused! Return to sender." Man, it felt good.

The next morning, before dropping them in the mail, I decided to check with the post office. I explained I was fed up by these unsolicited mailings.

"It's trash," the clerk said. "Throw it away."

"But I don't want to throw them away," I said. I tried to tell her about the landfills and the packaging and the bags of trash, but she cut me off.

"We will not deliver it, sir."

I called a second post office and got the same answer. The bulk-rate postage used by AOL and other mass mailers does not include return service. "Unfortunately, you'll have to get rid of them yourself," the clerk said.

I scoured the AOL Web site, thinking it must have information on how to return these unwanted disks at the company's expense. I clicked on "Discover All Things AOL" and discovered everything except how to give the cursed things back. I clicked on "spam" (after all, wasn't that what this was?), but again no luck.

Headed for the Trash

In my Internet searching, I discovered a group (www.nomore aolcds.com) dedicated to ending the wasteful practice of sending out millions of unsolicited CDs, many of which will end up in the trash. The California-based group is collecting unwanted AOL CDs, and when it has gathered one million, it plans to truck them to the company's headquarters in Virginia and dump them on the front steps. I want to be there for that.

I contemplated mailing the CDs back to AOL (22000 AOL Way, Dulles, Virginia, 20166). But why should I pay to return something I never asked for?

Finally, I found a toll-free number (1-800-466-5463) and quickly got through to a helpful AOL sales rep named Mike, who was eager to sign me up. When I told him I just wanted to be removed from the mailing list, he said, "Hold, please."

Of course, I was disconnected.

On my second call, after navigating a maze of automated prompts, I reached a polite man named Mbuso in South Africa. I never knew Pennsylvania could be pronounced so many ways. Mbuso took my information and promised that my days of receiving these ecological obscenities were behind me.

That still doesn't solve the problem of the two double-disk boxed sets cluttering my desk. Who knows, maybe I'll take up target shooting.

In a Flash, Life Is Ever So Fragile

I was standing at a busy intersection waiting for the light to change. Beside me stood a middle-aged woman and a gray-haired man. We were all about to glimpse our mortality.

It was evening rush hour, dusk was upon us, everyone was in a hurry. Traffic whizzed by inches from where we stood, staring across the street at the pedestrian signal.

When the light changed, each of us instinctively began to step off the curb. An instant later, we were all reeling back against each other. A delivery truck, trying to beat the light, sped past inches from the curb and through the intersection against a very, very, very red light.

The wind from the speeding truck slapped our faces. Another step and one or more of us would have been beneath the wheels.

"Lord!" the woman said.

"Yiii!" the man said.

"Wow!" I said. "That was close."

We were three strangers brought briefly, intensely, together in the faceless urban jungle, bonded by our shared close call with death.

We briefly counted our blessings, shook our heads in disbelief at the red-light runner, then hurried our separate ways.

Luckily, it was just a fleeting moment, soon shrugged off. Yet, I couldn't help but wonder, how many inches stood between close and catastrophe?

A Universal Truth

When I was a teenager, I read the novel *Things Fall Apart* by the African writer Chinua Achebe. It depicts a Nigerian tribal village, stable for centuries, that quickly and utterly crumbles after the arrival of colonialism. My close call spurred me to think again about that book and the universal truth in its title.

Things fall apart. In a heartbeat, they can and do. In a moment as innocuous and everyday as shoveling snow or plugging in a toaster or stepping off the curb to cross the street.

Last week, things fell apart close to home. The girl across the street, a sweet-natured, always smiling high school student who used to baby-sit my children, was driving a few miles from home. Just another routine trip until she came to a dip in the road where water tends to stand. Only on this day the temperature was well below freezing. One moment dry pavement, the next black ice. A life forever altered.

The girl I used to walk home beneath the stars remains hospitalized with brain injuries. A neighborhood waits and prays and, helpless to do anything more, makes endless casseroles as if food alone can turn back time and make a child whole again.

For Jose Varela and Blanca Santiago, fate found them as they slept in their home in Egg Harbor Township, outside Atlantic City. An SUV skidded off the pavement Friday, crashed through their bedroom wall, and landed on their bed, killing them both. Their three sons, who escaped injury, are left parentless.

Things fall apart, and sometimes in ways so incredible as to seem impossible. Except they are not.

Three Brothers

Two days after Varela and Santiago were killed in their sleep, three brothers left a pub near Macungie in western Lehigh County intent on doing the right thing. Earlier, knowing they would be drinking and not wanting to drive, they got a ride to the pub and planned to call a taxi at the end of the night, according to published accounts. But no taxi would come.

And so the brothers struck out on foot about 2:00 A.M. Sunday. A two-mile walk on a crisp December night. Nothing particularly harrowing there.

But as the brothers crossed Hamilton Boulevard, an SUV struck two of them. Stephen Polukard, thirty-four, of Lower

Macungie, and Michael Polukard, thirty-two, of Belford, New Jersey, were killed; Daniel Polukard, of Jackson, New Jersey, was unhurt.

Sometimes life can seem like a shooting gallery. We are the ducks; the shots come at random, picking off some, sparing others, with no pattern or predictability. And certainly with no fairness. Life is many things. Fair is not one of them.

And so I count my blessings as a teenage girl lies beneath her parents' gaze; as three children begin life without parents; as one brother prepares to bury the other two.

Things fall apart. For the rest of us, there is tomorrow.

Avoiding Shoals of Adolescence

Over the weekend, I sat my son down and gave him The Talk.

No, not the birds and the bees. Not the riot act on drinking and driving. Not drugs. Not sex. This was the "Life Is Like a Sailboat" talk.

The occasion was the arrival of his report card. It had its high points but its share of disappointments, too. My son needed to reorder his priorities.

"You know," I began, "life is a little like sailing a boat."

My father had given me the same talk one summer evening about thirty-five years ago as we skimmed along in the family dinghy on a quiet lake, the sails catching the gold of the sunset.

We were sailing along in silence when abruptly he began.

Life is like sailing a boat, he had told me, his hand on the tiller. Small, continual adjustments at the helm are needed to stay on course and eventually get where you need to go.

A good sailor, he pointed out, picks a clear destination on the far shore and sticks to it. No matter what weather kicks up, what obstacles and detours arise, he doesn't lose sight of his goal.

A good sailor watches for submerged rocks and other hazards along the way, giving them wide berth, he said. Blowing off course is one thing, running aground quite another. One is easily corrected, the other almost always irreversible.

A good sailor, Dad said, anticipates the winds of change before they strike. He watches for storm clouds and knows when to seek shelter and when to ride them out.

My father was not the most expansive man, and as suddenly as he had begun, he was done. A primer for life's complex journey summed up in a handful of basic sailing rules. I was thirteen and adrift myself, floating directionless in the sea of adolescence.

Lessons Repeated

Yet the lessons were so simple they sunk in. Stay on course. Steer clear of hazards. Make frequent little changes to avoid life's worst spills.

Now here I was, repeating the same drill to my own thirteen-year-old. Off I went, repeating my father's words from long ago nearly verbatim, wondering as I did if he, too, had stolen them from his father, or if I was the only generational plagiarist in the family.

Sailing is something my son and I share. He has felt the boat heel and lurch when he has overcorrected or, more often, failed to correct.

The sailboat—the same one I sailed with my father—was out of the water for the season, sitting in the backyard under a tarp, but the lessons of summer remained fresh.

Well-timed, nearly invisible corrections along the boat ride of life can make all the difference, I told him.

So I broke the bad news: We'd be making a few minor changes here aboard the SS *Middling Grades*. The video games would be going off until further notice; the personal computer would be used only for homework and research. Television, at least on school nights, would be curtailed.

Seeking Balance

I'm not the type to see evil in these things, not in moderation. But they had quietly crept into an ever-growing slice of my son's waking hours, even as he assured his parents he was staying on top of his responsibilities.

It's not the influence of video games and television that I worry about, but what they displace, not just time for homework and reading but for running and lollygaging, for playing Ping-Pong and kicking through piles of leaves. For being a boy.

We were making this small compass correction in order to keep our eyes on the dot on the horizon that is high school, and the dots of college and career beyond that, all leading to the ultimate destination at journey's end: a life lived fully and happily.

He started to protest but stopped himself. I think even he realized it was time to get back on course.

That night, we sat together at the kitchen table as he worked geometry problems and I looked helplessly on. (What ever happened to the old math?)

When he was done, with the distractions of video games and television out of the picture and nothing else pressing, I broke out the cookies and we sat at the table and talked and talked away. About nothing and everything. Just father-and-son stuff.

On the sailboat ride of life, there's something to be said for that, too.

⌒⌒⌒

Caught in the Midst of Wilma's Wild Winds

Call it bad luck; call it happenstance. Whatever the reasons, I found myself yesterday in a Westin Hotel in Fort Lauderdale, Florida, its doors tied shut with rope, trapped with about two hundred others directly in the path of Hurricane Wilma.

I had arrived over the weekend for a book-signing and knew right away this would be no ordinary visit. Flashing signs along Interstate 95 warned: "Mandatory evacuation of Florida Keys in progress."

The hotel staff handed out flashlights and water bottles. I went to bed Sunday night beneath calm, balmy skies.

At 7:00 A.M. I awoke to rain lashing the picture windows of my twelfth-floor room. I grabbed a pad of paper and began taking notes.

7:05 A.M.: I stand at my window looking out over Fort Lauderdale. Only a few cars are on I-95, and they're driving very fast. Across the city, I see occasional, spectacular bursts of blue-white light where power transformers short out followed immediately by entire neighborhoods going black.

7:18 A.M.: The power flicks off briefly. It occurs to me I have not yet made coffee. I rush to the coffeemaker, drop in the Starbucks pouch, hit the button. The machine has time to make one gurgle before the room and everything outside around me goes dark. Dawn is well past, but the sky is midnight black.

7:35 A.M.: I sit in the dark with my flashlight as the winds steadily build. I can feel the building rocking from side to side now.

8:10 A.M.: I hear a loud snap and see a large piece of siding fly past my window and crash to the ground. The room sways more noticeably. The wind speed looks as if it could be 90 m.p.h.

8:18 A.M.: A giant "W" flies past my window and crashes onto the flat roof several stories below me, crumpling as though it is made of tinfoil. I am now officially staying at the estin. An "i" soon follows. The building rattles, shakes and, oddly, moans. Palm trees are falling over cars in the parking lot. It's now darker outside than it was at 7:00.

8:49 A.M.: The phone rings. A hotel clerk says calmly but emphatically for me to come downstairs immediately. "The ballroom is the safest spot," he says. I will later learn that windows have begun to blow out of guests' rooms. In the hallway, the room doors rattle violently against their jambs as if the place is haunted.

8:51 A.M.: In the lobby, I'm shocked by the damage. The front door is blown out, broken glass scattered about. The marble and Italian tile floor, so sedately elegant the night before, is covered in water, leaves, and debris. A skylight is missing. Rain and wind whip through the lobby. It's like the Rainforest Café, only for real.

9:05 A.M.: It is a cliché of hurricane description, but one that is true. The wind outside roars like a freight train. Literally. It chugs and billows and snorts like a locomotive at full throttle.

9:22 A.M.: Inside the ballroom, the Westin staff serves eggs, bacon, and orange juice to guests and employees' families, many of whom have fled nearby homes and are here with pets. Dogs bark nervously. The Creole-speaking children of the Haitian maids and the English-speaking children of the moneyed guests play beautifully together, laughing and shrieking with excitement.

10:00 A.M.: The eye of the storm passes directly over us, and the winds, which had been topping 100 m.p.h., suddenly go still. "Don't go outside," a native Floridian warns. "The worst is still coming."

10:23 A.M.: He is right. The back wall of the hurricane hits us with a force that shakes the huge building. More trees fall. The word *awesome* is overused and misused, but on this morning it says everything. The storm is awesome, breathtaking in its ferocity and violence and relentless punishment. A second glass door blows out. The wind picks the water off the lobby floor as a single unit and hurls it horizontally.

11:09 A.M.: The strongest gusts yet, somewhere well above 110 m.p.h., slam the hotel. Treetops, twisted free of their trunks, dance across the pavement. Curtains from the breached rooms above tear free and billow through the sky like runaway spinnakers.

Noon: More free food. The Westin staff is wonderfully gracious. It's a Southern coastal tradition, one I first experienced while riding out Hurricane Andrew with my wife and an infant in 1992: Hurricane Hospitality. Now, we eat chicken fricassee and steamed asparagus under emergency-generator lights, strangers sitting together, chatting, bound by this shared predicament.

12:25 P.M.: I meet Michael Shofman, forty-five, a Russian immigrant who fled his apartment near the water. "I've been here seven years, and I've never seen anything like this," he says.

12:40 P.M.: The hurricane's final bands are nearly past us now. The winds drop below 100, then 80, then 60 m.p.h. The staff is already sweeping up glass and leaves and broken pots. This storm is no Katrina, no Andrew, not even close. And yet, it is humbling in its magnificence. I realize how seriously I had underestimated it.

1:00 P.M.: As quickly as it arrived, Wilma is gone, leaving in its wake at least six dead, massive power outages, widespread damage, and debris everywhere. Shofman, the Russian immigrant, steps outside through the shattered glass door, points to a brightening spot on the horizon, and proclaims loudly for all to hear, "God bless America!"

Time for Parents to Take the Wheel

Like most everyone, I like to be right. This is one time I wish I had been wrong.

On Monday, I wrote about the deaths of three Bucks County boys, all sixteen, in a speeding car that spun out of control on a lonely country road.

Despite the headlines, despite the steady stream of teenagers coming to the crash site to grieve, I predicted it would make no difference.

Those young drivers hardwired to speed were still going to speed. The ones convinced of their own invincibility would entertain no doubts. And more kids would end up in coffins.

"There are no lessons learned," I wrote. "Only more deaths and more shattered families."

Before the ink was even dry on that column, the prediction came true. No joy in that.

At 10:45 P.M. Sunday, it happened all over again. Same county. Same circumstances. Same awful, predictable outcome. More flowers and teddy bears piled in the rain by the side of the road for two more dead.

Another senseless, stupid shame.

As in the first accident, the driver of the car was reportedly speeding. None of the five occupants of the car wore a seat belt.

Ten days and thirty miles apart, history repeated itself, and no one was, or should have been, surprised.

Time to Wake Up

It made me wonder about the folly of trying to teach kids— not all kids, but a lot of them—to be something other than what they are: young and reckless and immature.

Maybe it is time we all just give up on the notion of teaching kids to slow down and drive safely. Maybe it's time we instead ask parents to wake up.

It is awkward to second-guess a parent who has just lost a child, and I do not mean any disrespect. God knows, tragedy can visit even the most cautious of homes.

But the question hangs there like a pall above the carnage of these two deadly wrecks, begging for an answer.

What were these newly minted drivers doing out at night in powerful, fast cars filled with other teens? In the first wreck, the driver was behind the wheel of a high-performance BMW. The second crash involved a Mustang, Ford's legendary muscle car.

Kids, cars, darkness, speed. It is a time-tested recipe for carnage. We all want to trust our kids, to believe in their good judgment. But can any parent honestly tell himself or herself that this is a good idea?

In the first crash, on Township Line Road separating Hilltown and New Britain Townships, the driver had received his license exactly one day earlier, and yet there he was behind the wheel, unsupervised, with friends. Does anyone seriously believe that slim piece of plastic overnight made him competent and mature enough to handle that intoxicating temptation?

Mom's Rule

Parents, the time has come to stop pleading with our kids and start telling them the way it's going to be.

Let me tell you about a totally uncool and unreasonable parent who did just that. She had a strict rule, on which she refused to relent, even by the time her fourth child reached driving age. That child was me.

Moms rule: No driving anywhere without a parent in the car for one full year. On your seventeenth birthday, you were given more freedom, but still not permission to drive after dark with a bunch of friends in the car.

My siblings and I all complained bitterly about the unfairness of her rule. We pointed out how all the other kids got to drive unsupervised as soon as they had their licenses.

Her stock response: "If they all jumped off a bridge, would you jump off, too? Just because you have a license doesn't mean you're ready to be out there on your own."

Even then, despite my hot protests, I knew she was right. I knew I wasn't ready. And she gave me the excuse I needed to just say no. No to the temptation; no to the peer pressure.

When all else fails, blame it on Mom. I did, and I'm here to tell the tale. Some of my classmates were not so lucky.

So how about it, parents? Are we brave enough to be uncool and unreasonable and totally square in our children's eyes? It's a small price to pay to keep them alive.

Just Fill 'Er Up with Cooking Oil

When gasoline prices topped $3 a gallon recently, Samuel Yoder couldn't help smiling.

Instead of paying dearly at the pump, he did what he's been doing for the last two years. He pulled his 1985 Mercedes-Benz sedan up to his barn in Berks County and filled it from a fifty-five-gallon drum of used cooking oil. Total cost of fill-up: zero.

That would be $0.00. Who could blame him for being a little gleeful?

It's not that Yoder, forty-five, takes joy in other people's pain, but he hopes soaring fuel prices will serve as a wake-up call for gas-guzzling Americans.

Yoder believes America's thirst for foreign oil will be its downfall, and he is walking the talk. He bought the used diesel

Mercedes for $2,000 two years ago in Philadelphia and paid $1,000 more for a German-made converter kit that allows the car to burn any combination of diesel fuel and vegetable cooking oil. Except in the cold winter months, he burns vegetable oil nearly exclusively.

What thrills him most is that his fuel supplier is not a tyrannical foreign country that houses anti-American terrorists. It is a local restaurant that is happy to give him all the used peanut oil he can use. Otherwise, it would have to pay to have it hauled away.

Hidden Treasure

"I pick up anywhere from five to ten gallons a week," he says as he holds up a jug of the golden oil. "It's so cool. I take a raw product that's already been used and is going to go to a landfill, and I'm using it as a fuel source."

Not only that, but the oil is homegrown in the United States by U.S. farmers. And it burns 60 percent cleaner than regular diesel fuel. When he starts his car, the exhaust coming from the tailpipe smells like French fries.

Yoder and his wife, Annemarie, make their living as veterinarians in Kutztown, but it is on their eighty-eight-acre Berks County farm, which they share with their twin five-year-old daughters, that their passion lies. It's the farm Yoder grew up on and where his Pennsylvania German father instilled lessons of frugality and self-sufficiency.

Now the couple are working to become fully self-sufficient.

Yoder walks me around the farm as the sun sets behind the tree line. I meet the chickens that supply fresh eggs and the goat that provides a gallon of fresh milk each morning. In the pasture are draft horses that pull the plows through the fields, where the couple grow the grains needed to feed all their animals, including pigs and cattle raised for meat.

A Self-Contained System

Near the house is an organic garden, where the family grows most of the vegetables it will eat all year, and a sun-powered dryer for preserving them. The garden is fertilized with the manure from the farm's animals.

Inside, the house is outfitted with high-efficiency appliances and heated with wood.

But the most obvious sign that this is no ordinary farm are the giant banks of solar-collection cells, some mounted on poles, some on the barn roof, that greet you as you pull into the driveway. Even on overcast days, the collectors are able to convert the sun's energy into electricity for the house and farm.

On bright, sunny days, the Yoders often produce more electricity than they use, and they have a two-way meter that allows them to bank kilowatt credits with their local power company.

The photovoltaic system cost the couple a whopping $40,000, but it has no moving parts and they expect it to give them reliable, free electricity for the rest of their lives.

"It'll probably take me twenty years to pay it off," Yoder says. "But it's the principle. I put my money where my mouth is."

The Yoders are putting their money behind their principles in another way. They and a group of volunteers have organized the two-day Renewable Energy and Sustainable Living Festival. It takes place at Kempton Community Center in Kempton with booths, workshops, lectures, and children's activities aimed at winning converts to an energy-sustainable lifestyle. (For more information: www.paenergyfest.com.)

Yoder is hoping the festival will become an annual event.

"We're trying to show people this can be done," he said. "This works. I'm living proof that it works."

"It's Never the Same": Too True

I was running late.

At the end of the long hallway, the last room on the right sat empty.

The bed was made, a walker in the corner. My mother and her wheelchair were missing.

I found a nurse. "I'm Ruth Grogan's son. Is my mother around?"

It was a dumb question. This was a nursing home. Of course she was around. Everyone was always around.

"I'd try the chapel," the nurse offered. "Mass started at eleven."

Life has its chapters, distinct divisions marked by watershed events, and this summer marked a new one in mine. A year earlier, when I had visited my aging parents at their home outside Detroit, ripe tomatoes lined the windowsill, a pot of soup simmered on the stove, and my folks greeted me happily at the door.

This summer's visit marked a new beginning. As my children swam in the lake I had swum in as a boy, I sifted through my father's papers, visited his grave, and spent time with my mother in the place she now calls home.

As far as nursing homes go, it's a lovely one, perched on a shaded hill overlooking a lake and run by kind nuns committed to compassionate care. But it is still a nursing home with all the smells and sounds and sadness nursing homes hold.

I made my way down corridors lined with frail women passing the hours. "Take me with you," one of them pleaded as I passed.

Bowed White Heads

In the chapel, an ancient priest celebrated Mass before a small clutch of nuns and about three dozen patients, their wheelchairs arranged in an arc around the altar. From behind, the bowed white heads all looked alike. As I scanned the congregants, I realized nearly all of them were asleep. My mother was no exception.

I touched her shoulder and whispered, "Hi, Ruthie." Her eyes opened and widened with surprise. She had forgotten I was coming.

My eighty-nine-year-old mother's memory has been fleeing her for some years now. When my father died in December, she lost not only her husband of fifty-eight years but a devoted and exceptionally attentive 24/7 caregiver.

Mom's eyes shut again, and I stood with my hands on her shoulders as the priest soldiered on. At Communion, he walked down the rows of wheelchairs, placing wheat hosts onto tongues. My mother woke to accept hers and, as she always has, pressed a fist to her heart and began working her lips in silent prayer.

Some things are not easily lost.

After Mass, I wheeled her into the courtyard, where she tilted her head toward the sun and smiled. Deep lines crossed her face, and her hair was as snowy as a blizzard. But a child's face looked up at me, a little girl lost in her innocence.

A Song from Long Ago

She began to hum and then sing. It was a song I had never heard before, a ditty about a brash child swallowed by an alligator she thought she could tame. Mom had no idea what she had eaten for breakfast that morning, but she reeled effortlessly through the stanzas, not missing a beat.

"Where did you learn that?" I asked.

"Girl Scouts," she said.

I had to laugh. "That was eighty years ago! It's about time you sang it to me." Then she sang it all over again.

We sat quietly for a moment. She broke the silence with an observation.

"Once they leave home, that's it," she volunteered as if she were telling it to someone other than one of those who had left. "They come back to visit, but it is never the same."

I wanted to insist otherwise, but she was right. It never is. It never was.

I wheeled her back to her room and kissed her goodbye.

"I'll be back this evening with Jenny and the kids," I told her. What I did not say is that the next morning we would be returning to Pennsylvania.

Outside in the parking lot, I looked back through her room window where I had left her. She was peering out at something far, far away. When I caught her attention, a startled look of pleasant surprise came across her face, the same look she had given me at chapel. It was as if she were seeing me for the first time.

"Aw, Mom," I whispered.

She blew me a kiss. I blew one back, then drove away.

When First Class Turns Low Class

Ladies and gentlemen, we now interrupt this flight to announce that, no, this is not Mississippi. And, no, the year is not 1964. Just thought you'd want to know that.

In the United States of America in 2005, it is easy to believe the country's ugly racial past is light years behind us. De facto segregation still exists, most notably in many schools and churches. Still, the chasm narrows each year. The black middle and professional classes are robust and growing. African Americans are prominently represented in all fields, from law to government to medicine. Our children increasingly mix—on playgrounds and sports teams, at summer camp and the mall— in ways their parents did not.

As a society, we like to think we have moved past the dark days of blatant, in-your-face racial antipathy.

Then comes along a guy like Robert Baldwin, a self-employed engineer from Blue Bell in Montgomery County, to toss cold water on our comfortable assumptions.

Baldwin was seated with his wife and adult son in first class on a U.S. Airways flight from Los Angeles to Philadelphia. Directly in front of him was another area couple, E. Steven Collins, a radio executive and on-air personality, and his wife, Lisa.

Nothing too unusual there. Two professional couples, both from the same region. You might expect them to pass the flight in friendly conversation. Think again.

Baldwin is white; the Collinses black. And that, for Baldwin, appeared to be a big, big issue.

Philadelphia police reported that Baldwin began muttering racial epithets at the couple. Then he began kicking the backs of their seats. Then he placed his feet on the headrest of Lisa Collins' seat and shoved them between the seats to rest them on the armrest.

"I didn't know if I was dealing with a terrorist or a lunatic," Collins told the *Inquirer*'s Vernon Clark last week.

Or a developmentally arrested preschooler. All of the above?

The flight attendant attempted to intervene without luck. Baldwin allegedly used the N-word, apparently seething that nonwhites would be allowed to fly in first class.

Wouldn't want them lowering the high standards of seat-kicking, epithet-hurling decorum now, would we?

Baldwin's behavior became so obnoxious, his own son reportedly told him to quit acting like a child.

Police arrested Baldwin in the baggage-claim area, and he was later charged with felony ethnic intimidation and misdemeanor assault and harassment.

Charges of impersonating a yahoo in the first degree may be pending.

To Collins' credit, he did not inflame the situation. (Yes, sir, you were within your rights to deck the little gnat once you stepped off the plane.)

Baldwin, forty-seven, still awaits his day in court. Who knows, he might have a perfectly good explanation. (Altitude-induced flailing-leg syndrome? A really violent reaction to airline food?)

But the other day I stared long and hard at his police mug shot—the piercing blue eyes, the grimacing frown—and tried to understand the hatred of which he stands accused.

What did this man have to be so angry about? The most virulent racism often is found in those whites of the underclass who have accomplished little with their lives and need a scapegoat to blame.

Yet this man appears successful. He lives in a desirable zip code, in a home he paid more than a half million dollars for in 2001. What gives?

I called his home Friday to ask him about the incident. To ask him what deep well the racial hatred he is accused of sprang from?

The phone was out of service.

So let me presume to speak for white people—at least the vast majority of us—and tell Lisa and E. Steven Collins that we are mortified and embarrassed by this behavior. We thought, as a race, we had moved past this ugly point. We might have been wrong.

The incident in the skies over America last week is a chafing reminder of how far we all still have to go.

～⌒◌

A Life Extended by a Generous Gift

Jim Gleason knows something about human generosity.

He is the recipient of what he calls "the ultimate act of kindness."

Thirteen years ago, Gleason was a hard-driven information-technology manager in the Philadelphia suburbs when he was laid flat by a bad virus.

No big deal. Everyone gets the occasional bug.

But this one was different, and by the time Gleason found his way to a hospital, his life was in jeopardy. The virus had attacked his heart, and only a third of it was still functioning.

The father of three began a regimen of medications, but by 1994, his heart had wasted away to 18 percent functionality. At age fifty-one, he was among the walking dead.

Doctors admitted him to the Hospital of the University of Pennsylvania and put him on a heart-transplant list. There he waited, finding himself in the odd position of hoping for a healthy stranger's untimely death.

Seven weeks into his wait, the phone call came. It was the hospital's transplant coordinator. "He said, 'Jim, I think we found a heart for you,'" Gleason, of Beverly, Burlington County, recalled yesterday.

An athletic man, who Gleason would later learn worked as a New York prison employee, was celebrating his thirty-eighth birthday on the streets of Brooklyn when he was attacked with a baseball bat.

A Coma, Then Death

"He ended up in a coma, and ten days later he was declared brain-dead," Gleason said. In their grief, the man's siblings agreed to donate his organs. A few hours later, Gleason had a new heart—and life.

The next day he was up and walking around, and within weeks he again had the stamina of a young man.

Years passed. Gleason could not forget the family that gave him life, nor the man whose heart beat in his chest. "He's with me all the time, and I mean that in a very real sense," Gleason said.

Then in 2002, at a gathering of transplant recipients and donor families, it happened. Gleason, who had dug through records to learn the identity of his donor, met the brother of Roberto Cuebas, the man whose heart became his own.

"There is no way words can explain," Gleason said, describing the emotion of the moment. "You are looking at a person who saved your life. He lost his brother; he didn't know who I was. And still he said yes to organ donation.

"I asked him why, and he said, 'It just made sense. What else would I do? Bury the organs in the ground?' He said his brother was a very giving man, and he knew if he had a choice he would have said yes."

Gleason, his eyes brimming, hugged Gilberto Cuebas for a long moment. Two strangers, one shared miracle.

From loss, life. From sorrow, solace. And gratitude of the deepest order.

"It's beyond description," Gleason said. "You can only imagine."

A New Chapter

More years passed. In February, Gleason was laid off from his management job. He was separated from his wife, his children were grown. He began his own volunteer enterprise, speaking to recent heart recipients, who sometimes have trouble adjusting to life after near-death.

"My basic message is life can be whatever you want it to be," he said. "You're not disabled anymore."

And he is once again in love, to another volunteer. When his divorce is final, he said, he plans to marry her.

Her name is Pam Colvell, and she is what people in the world of organ transplants know as "a donor mom."

In 1997, her thirteen-year-old son, Christopher, was struck by a car as he rode his bicycle home from cutting his grandfather's lawn. The next day, after doctors declared him brain-dead, she donated her son's organs to others who could not live without them.

A grieving mother's ultimate gift.

The human heart beats bravely on.

Kindness Can Be Contagious

"He would give you the shirt off his back."

Anne Kubach of Collegeville had often heard the expression to describe an exceptionally generous person. But she never believed anyone literally would do such a thing. Then her son, Dan, a criminal justice major at Shippensburg University, went to Florida on spring break this year. Now she knows.

Dan was walking to catch a bus with his friends when the strap on one of his sandals broke. He told his friends to go on without him. Just then another young man whom he did not know stepped forward and asked Dan his shoe size. Kubach said the stranger then took off his shoes and handed them over.

"He refused payment or an offer to meet up later so the shoes could be returned," Kubach said. "It just seemed like a 'wow!' moment, and one we are still impressed with."

Her story is just one of the dozens that have rolled in from *Inquirer* readers who have experienced charitable acts, large and small, that restored their faith in the human race.

An eighty-year-old widow in Cherry Hill wrote to gush about the young couple across the street who constantly look out for her.

Donna Hart of Merion Station requires an electric wheelchair to get around and said she is constantly amazed at the generosity of strangers, including—this is not a misprint—SEPTA bus drivers. "Never in my wildest imaginings did I ever expect to be the recipient of so much kindness," Hart wrote. "I feel like I have a constant guardian angel with me."

Roadside Shining Knights

I heard from many women who, stranded on the side of the road with dead batteries or flat tires, were rescued by strangers—"kind gentlemen," as several of the damsels in distress put it. Who said chivalry was dead?

I heard about strangers who went out of their way to return lost wallets, cell phones, credit cards, even cash. Norman Cowell of Marlton accidentally tipped his airport driver $70, thinking he was handing him several singles; the driver, knowing it had to be a mistake, chased him down and returned the money.

Marian Pelton of Havertown ordered a bagel and coffee only to discover her wallet was empty. The cashier simply told her to pay on her next visit, "not knowing if she'd ever see me again," said Pelton, who returned the money later the same day.

Sometimes a little trust goes a long way.

Clair Hoifjeld, a semiretired clergyman from Wyncote, was handling estate business in Fort Lee, New Jersey, several weeks ago after the death of a relative. "Several vital documents, along with considerable cash and other important items, were in my briefcase which, in my state of mind, I accidentally left on the curb when we loaded our car," he wrote.

When Hoifjeld arrived home and discovered the briefcase missing, he was heartsick. But a message was waiting on his answering machine. A man had found the briefcase and said he would keep it safe until Hoifjeld could return for it. "I tried hard to get him to accept a reward," Hoifjeld wrote, "but he politely refused, saying, 'I'm just going to sleep better, knowing I did what I should have done.'"

A Long, Hot Wait

One of my favorite stories, because it showed the contagious nature of kindness, came from Stephanie Barberra of Skippack Township, who found herself one hot afternoon waiting in an interminably long line at the Department of Motor Vehicles.

"I had done my hard time of fifty minutes, when in walked a young mother with two very young children," Barberra wrote. The mother was trying unsuccessfully to occupy the fussy children, and Barberra, the mother of a toddler herself, began to feel for her. When Barberra's number was called, she turned and handed it to the young mother.

"It was as if I had offered her a winning lottery ticket," Barberra wrote. "She thanked me repeatedly. It felt really good."

Now the best part: As Barberra settled in to wait another hour, a young man whose number had just been called turned to her and said, "Go ahead." Proving once again that one good deed deserves another.

Kindness Comes in Unlikely Places

Simple acts of human kindness can be found in the least likely places.

Dan Brennan of West Chester found it in the intensive-care unit of a St. Louis hospital after his brother was critically injured in a car accident.

As Brennan kept a round-the-clock vigil, a food-filled cooler mysteriously appeared beside him. "Not just snack foods but cold cuts, bread, condiments and more," he recalled.

"There was no name on the cooler." The nurses told him a woman had left it. "That gift sustained me through one of the most difficult times of my life," he wrote.

Maria McCormick of Upper Darby found it in a Wawa store in Sea Isle City while visiting the Shore. The store was jammed, with a long line at the register. McCormick noticed the man behind her had three young children with him, and she offered to let him go ahead of her, which he did.

"When I got to the front of my line, the cashier told me [the bill] was already paid for by the man with the children," McCormick wrote. "I couldn't believe it! I got outside just in time to thank him for being so kind. His response was that I was the one who was being kind by letting him in front of me in the first place."

Candy Lerner of Philadelphia found it at 2:30 A.M. when she was awakened by the repeated ring of her doorbell. When she and her husband looked outside, a man was holding the keys to their house. Lerner's husband had accidentally left them dangling from the front door, and the passing motorist spotted them. "We thanked him and he was quickly on his way," she wrote. "I can think of many things that could have happened if he hadn't noticed them and rung our bell."

A Group Effort

Gayle Payne found it in the parking lot of the Costco near her home in Mount Laurel, where a small-built man who spoke very little English was trying without luck to wrestle a large-screen television he had just purchased into his vehicle. "A strong young man with a large truck changed course and came over to offer his truck and his help," Payne said. Others joined him and together the group of strangers heaved and lifted the

240-pound TV into the young man's truck. He then followed the owner home to deliver it. "None would accept any money," Payne reported. (And no, you skeptics, the guy with the truck didn't speed off in the opposite direction with a free TV.)

Chuck Johnson of Philadelphia found it on Lombard Street last week when he spotted a pedestrian pausing mid-stride to pick up someone else's litter. Johnson was so appreciative he stopped and shook the man's hand.

"He just tossed off the thanks by saying he does it all the time," Johnson said. "Just imagine . . . if every day each person in Philly picked up one small piece of litter. What an amazing difference that would make."

Alone and Stranded

Sandy Guydon of Philadelphia found kindness on the Schuylkill Expressway near King of Prussia when she ran out of gas. "I didn't have a cell phone, and I sat there for three to four hours while cars zipped by," she wrote. "Finally a car with two women and several children stopped." The women returned with a can of gasoline, and then followed Guydon to the nearest gas station. "They wouldn't take any money," she said. "I can't begin to tell you how grateful I was."

Marie Drennen of Oxford found it in her own home when her daughters, Devin, eleven, and Amanda, thirteen, each received $300 for Christmas from their grandparents—and each decided, without parental prompting, to donate the full amount to tsunami relief efforts.

And, finally, Craig TenBroeck of Radnor found kindness, and something more, on a lonely road outside Halifax, Nova

Scotia, while on vacation with his wife, Jill. The couple were hopelessly lost and asked a stranger for directions to their hotel.

"He said, 'Come on, I'll show you the way,' and he drove us right to our hotel's parking lot," TenBroeck recalled. "It probably took him miles out of his way. He walked back to our car and we thanked him profusely and said 'God bless you.' He turned back to us and said, 'Since you said that, could I ask you to pray for me? I have cancer.' We, of course, said we would, and we did, for many days."

On Monday, the "Kindess Chronicles" continue.

Acts of Kindness Are All Around Us

The depressing headlines continue to roll in: "Boy Killed in Home-Invasion Attack" . . . "Man Fatally Shot after Being Thrown from Car."

And yet the quiet acts of human decency still manage to percolate up through the mire.

A week ago, I asked readers to share their true stories of unexpected kindness and charity from strangers. More than a hundred of you have responded so far, with new stories arriving daily, reminding me that, despite the inhumanity around us, basic human goodness is alive and kicking.

Some of the kind acts came during a crisis, such as a car accident or medical emergency. Most involved tiny everyday moments, such as the store clerk who ran out in a downpour to catch a customer who had left her purchase behind.

Or the woman who lost a $20 bill at a public pool, only to later find it waiting for her, turned in to a lifeguard.

Many of those I heard from referred to the person who helped them as "my angel." I kind of like that. Now, let the "Kindness Chronicles" begin.

Picking Up the Tab

Lynn Brandsma, an assistant professor of psychology at Chestnut Hill College, still remembers the Valentine's Day eight years ago when her boyfriend (now husband) proposed to her in a restaurant in Ardmore. "He had arranged ahead of time for the wait staff to come out with roses and an Italian wedding cake," she recalled. "The entire restaurant applauded."

When the couple went to leave, their waiter told them that another customer already had paid their tab.

"We were not wealthy people. My husband had saved for months for that night," she said. "I cannot tell you how grateful we were to this man. He was with his wife and another couple and waved us off and wished us luck and said he hoped we were as happy in our marriage as he was in his."

Brandsma added: "Not a Valentine's Day goes by that I do not think of this man and silently thank him for what he did for us."

Speaking of unexpected generosity, John Roddy of Devon wrote: "Not too long ago on a cold winter night, my wife and I boarded a New York City bus around 10:00 P.M., not knowing that we needed the exact fare." Just as they were about to step back off the bus, "a kind lady got up from her seat and deposited two tokens for us in the coin box. She subsequently refused any payment from us. So much for stereotypical mean-spirited New Yorkers!"

A Bad Spill

Sandra Herman, fifty-seven, a bicycling enthusiast from Bensalem, was out for a ride on Bensalem Avenue earlier this month when she lost control on loose gravel, falling and striking her head on a guard rail. Her helmet prevented a serious injury, but she was dazed and scraped up. "Not ten seconds later, a gentleman stopped. He asked a million times if I was OK," Herman said. "He helped me get up . . . picked up my bike and drove me home. I never even thought to get his name."

Mia Hughes of Springfield, Delaware County, was on her way to a sports banquet with her daughter when her car tire went flat. She had no idea how to fix it and knew they did not have time to wait for a tow truck. Just then a car pulled up and a retiree got out and cheerfully changed the tire for her.

"All I know about this man is that he drove a grey Mustang and lived in Aldan," Hughes wrote. "But he was my angel for the day. We made it to the banquet on time, thanks to him."

Sharon Potts of Glenside was returning from a vacation in Oregon, where her son lives, and tried to board her flight with a carry-on bag filled with specimen rocks she had collected. The bag was deemed too large to carry on, and there was no time to check it. The gate agent told her she had to discard the stones or miss the flight.

"I was near tears, but out of the blue a woman who was seeing off her young son heard our plight and offered to take them back to my son's house so he could mail them to me," she wrote. The trip took the woman miles out of her way, but she refused Potts' offer of money. "Not life-saving or anything, but this stranger came to my rescue and had nothing to gain."

And the stories keep rolling in.

Pretty amazing.

Laws No Match for Junk Food Love

All across the country, our beloved junk food is under attack.

Schools are pulling it off lunch menus. Offices are booting it from vending machines. Public service announcements are urging us to just say no.

In Detroit, the mayor wants to slap a 2 percent surcharge (on top of the 6 percent sales tax) on anything sold in a fast-food restaurant.

In New York, an assemblyman has proposed a 1 percent tax on that holy trinity of popular culture—junk food, video games, and TV commercials—to fund anti-obesity programs.

Here in Philadelphia, City Councilwoman Blondell Reynolds Brown is more worried about potbellies than potholes. Last week she proposed an ordinance requiring fast food joints to hand out flyers listing the ingredients and nutritional values of its menu items.

Yeah, right, like that's going to work. Can't you just see thousands of Philly fast-food patrons suddenly scrutinizing the fine print that comes with their triple-bypass cheesesteaks. ("Good Lord, Edith, I had no idea eating a wheelbarrow-sized portion of deep-fried potatoes was fattening. Mama always told me to eat my vegetables!")

It Wasn't My Fault

And, as with all good things, the lawyers have gotten involved. If you're fat and love junk food, you just might be an unwitting victim of those greedy merchants of deep-fried death. Yes, they seduced you into eating all those supersized combos day after day, knowing full well they were turning you into a human dirigible.

And when Joe Junkfood takes the witness stand, tears running down his cheeks, he will say something like this: "I swear I never would have eaten three double-bacon cheeseburgers a day for the last fifteen years had I known this wasn't a balanced and nutritious diet. If only the restaurant had offered me carrot sticks as an alternative, I'd be svelte as a model."

It's gotten bad enough that sixteen states have passed laws protecting restaurants and other junk-food purveyors from these types of suits, and twenty-six state legislatures, including Pennsylvania and New Jersey, are weighing similar protections.

It's a little hard to muster sympathy for an adult who somehow never figured out that a near-exclusive diet of burgers, fries, and milkshakes isn't the best recipe for a long and lean life.

Protecting children from empty calories has more merit—after all, kids are supposed to be clueless—but even here the feel-good efforts to swap dastardly junk foods for "healthy alternatives" are largely a joke.

Take the effort to replace sodas with fruit juices. What parent wouldn't love such a calorie-smart switch.

Instead of a Pepsi, let them swig down a delicious cranberry-apple juice drink, with no added sweetener.

It sounds great—until you read the label. Fruit juices are virtually all sugar.

A Little Moderation

According to the USDA, cranberry-apple juice gets 100 percent of its calories from sugar, a teeth-grinding 23 grams in a six-ounce serving. Six ounces of Pepsi, by comparison, contains 20.25 grams. (The fruit juice does provide Vitamin C, which the soft drink does not.)

I'm feeling healthier already!

It's all a little silly. How much longer before some innovative politician proposes a Bureau of the Plump Posterior to regulate the nation's growing girth?

Living in a free country has countless benefits. It also has a price of admission: personal responsibility. And that requires moderation and will power.

Which brings us to the new, fifteen-pound hamburger. Where else, but in the Land of Very Large Eaters?

Yep, Pennsylvania.

Denny's Beer Barrel Pub in Clearfield, west of State College, already has a six-pounder, but the $39.95 monster "Belly Buster" apparently is aimed at the man who has everything, including a death wish.

Eat the whole thing in one five-hour sitting, and you get a free T-shirt, according to the *Pittsburgh Post-Gazette.*

You gotta love this place.

So what's it going to be, people? Belly Busters and extra-extra large T-shirts, or a little self-restraint?

One thing for certain: With the naked Zorro streaker still on the loose in the 'burbs and hanging it all out there—and with the cops fretting about copycats—we all have a stake in a more toned populace.

Dried tofu wafer anyone?

Bearing the Cost of Child-Bearing

When Kate Gosselin finally picks up the phone on the tenth ring, she sounds a little frazzled, and who can blame her?

From the background come the cries, shrieks, and whoops of babies. Six of them, to be exact.

The Berks County woman once feared she was unable to conceive. Today, thanks to fertility drugs, she has more children than she and her husband, Jonathan, know what to do with. Those would be twin four-year-old girls followed by the sextuplets, who turned one on May 10.

Gosselin's supercharged fertility is miraculous in its own right, a testament to the wonders—and pitfalls—of modern medicine. She has rocketed into the public spotlight, however, not for her baby-making prowess but for her insistence that she cannot mother alone.

The harried mom wants help—and she wants taxpayers to pick up the tab.

Because the fragile babies were born prematurely, Medicaid paid to provide a skilled home nurse thirty hours a week. But the babies are now robust, and Medicaid pulled the plug this month on paying for the nurse the Gosselins have come to rely on as "a second mommy."

Special Circumstances

The couple, who live in Wyomissing, have appealed that ruling, and on Thursday the mother will argue that her special circumstances—eight little ones and a husband who is gone twelve hours a day for his state-government job ninety minutes away in Harrisburg—merit taxpayer help. The state continues to pay for nurse Angie Krall while the appeal is pending.

"We did not ask for sextuplets. We wanted one last baby," Gosselin tells me, quickly adding that she loves all six beyond words. "We took the risk and we lost."

As you might imagine, her request has not gone over well. Angry letters have popped up in newspapers across Pennsylvania. Gosselin, a registered nurse, knew the risks of taking fertility drugs. Even after delivering twins on the first go-round, she rolled the dice again. And now she wants the state to pay for her gamble?

"People are very harsh to us, and I understand that," she says. "But until you walk exactly in my shoes and know my day-to-day life, it is very difficult to imagine. . . ."

I want to sympathize with her. Every parent knows how demanding and exhausting even one baby can be. But the more she talks, the more I find her to be inflexible.

I agree with her that she can't do it alone, but I ask why she needs an expensive skilled nurse instead of a basic child-care helper. Her only explanation is that she and the children have bonded with their nurse, and she'd hate to change now. She concedes the children no longer require specialized nursing care, and adds, "On Jon's income, we couldn't afford to pay someone even $6 an hour."

Paying for Child Care?

And that leads to another question. If money is so tight, why doesn't she return to work and enroll the children in day care? Nope. The family minivan cannot carry all eight children in one trip, and the couple can't afford a bigger van, she says. Besides, "I would be taking my paycheck and giving it to the day care." Welcome to the world of working parents.

She says family members live too far away or are too busy to help, and the stream of volunteers that came in the early months compromised the family's privacy. "There is no one," she says definitively. "I have racked my brain."

I have one other idea for her. The couple's house has about $100,000 of equity in it, she has estimated. Why don't they take out a loan to pay for the nurse themselves, just as parents do to pay for tuition or orthodontics? She doesn't want to do that, either.

She promises she wants Medicaid to pay for the nurse for only one more year, and by then the couple will be able to handle their brood on their own.

Obviously, society has a vested interest in making sure these eight children—all children—are properly nurtured. The question is whether taxpayers should be expected to take on a couple's burden. And if so, which couples, and for how long?

There are no easy answers, only an unsettling awareness that parenting, with all its joys and challenges, belongs ultimately to parents.

Give Mother Help for Children's Sake

I have been tossing and turning in bed lately. It's the sextuplets. Their sweet little faces haunt me.

They did not ask for this. They did not ask for the wrath rained down upon their family by angry Pennsylvanians, many of them mothers themselves. They did not seek the public-relations nightmare their parents, Kate and Jonathan Gosselin, brought on by setting themselves up for a mega-family they could not support—and then asking taxpayers to foot the bill for a Medicaid home nurse to help.

The Gosselins did this to themselves. They used fertility drugs, not once, but twice. They knew the risks and knew they could not bring themselves to selectively reduce the number of embryos. Is it any wonder the reaction, as I wrote last week, was so decidedly unsympathetic?

When I interviewed the mother, she radiated a sense of entitlement and inflexibility, prompting other mothers across the region to scold in surround sound: You made your decision, now live with it.

Many used the same expression: "Start taking responsibility for your own actions."

That's all fine and good—except that six innocent and defenseless children hang in the balance.

I should be snoozing soundly at night, but I see their faces. (You can view photos of the sextuplets at www.sixgosselins .com).

One Now Gone

In the dark, I see the face of another baby, too—one who did not make it.

Her name was Raya Donagi, and she also caught the nation's attention. Born with Down syndrome, she lived six months before her desperately despondent mother answered the voices in her head and slit the baby's throat.

Mine Ener, a distinguished professor at Villanova University, then committed suicide in jail.

It was a senseless, horrific tragedy filled with a parade of what-ifs.

What if she had only asked for help?

What if she had not tried to carry this burden alone?

What if she simply had dropped Raya at a fire station and walked away?

And now we have the Gosselins, doing exactly what so many of us belatedly asked of Mine Ener and other mothers who have snapped, such as Andrea Yates, the Texas woman who drowned her five children in a tub.

Why didn't they just ask for help?

Kate Gosselin is asking—admittedly in a clumsy, ham-fisted way that sounds self-serving and breeds resentment instead of compassion—but asking nonetheless.

And we have answered with a collective cold shoulder. We excoriate her as a free-loader and something less than a virtuous mother.

Do we punish the Gosselin children because their parents are not more skilled at fostering public sympathy?

And if something terrible were to happen, what would we say then? Oh, I guess they really did need help.

Recipe for Meltdown

I am not suggesting the Gosselins are on the verge of desperate acts. But they have brought upon themselves the makings of a desperate situation—a husband with a modest income and a three-hour round-trip commute; a mother at home with six one-year-olds and twin four-year-olds. It's a recipe for meltdown.

Kate Gosselin's request to have Medicaid continue to provide a skilled home nurse for another year is ridiculous. The once-fragile children are now robust; they do not need a nurse. Besides, Gosselin is a registered nurse herself.

But the harried mother definitely needs a helper or two. Or three.

They could be doting grandmothers or empty-nesters. They could be attentive high schoolers or college students looking to fill a community-service requirement.

It may take a village to raise sextuplets, but it doesn't take Medicaid.

Here's one other suggestion: What about the many anti-abortion protesters who spend countless hours picketing abortion clinics? How refreshing if instead they exchanged their pickets for Pampers and showed up at the Gosselins' home, ready to help. Wouldn't that be a more productive use of their time and energy?

After all, if they are truly committed to helping protect innocent lives, where better to start?

～

A Helping Hand, a Helping of Grace

After December's tsunami claimed countless thousands of lives and left millions more homeless, many Americans opened their checkbooks.

The Reverend Stanley Hagberg packed a sleeping bag, kissed his wife goodbye, and caught a flight into the heart of darkness.

For two months, Hagberg, a conservative Baptist minister from Hatboro, slogged through muck and debris on the Indonesian island of Sumatra, helping in any way he could.

He carried sacks of rice, delivered cooking oil, shoveled mud out of homes, painted flood-stained classrooms. Mostly, he listened as grief-stricken villagers who had lost everything— their homes, their livelihoods, their children—bared their souls. "Everyone had a story to tell," said Hagberg, sixty-six, who arrived back in Philadelphia last month.

The territory of Aceh on the northern tip of Sumatra, where he arrived February 7, was the closest landfall to the earthquake that spawned the tsunami that struck on December 26. A wall of water estimated at a hundred feet tall slammed the western coastline, wiping out everything in its path. The official casualty count was 126,000 dead and 40,000 missing, but Hagberg said locals believe the numbers to be far higher.

"As far as the eye could see in all directions, it was just nothing but leveled foundations," he said last week from his office at the Normandy Farms Estates retirement community in Blue Bell, where he is chaplain.

A Higher Calling

When the call had come asking him to join a Baptist relief mission to the devastated area, Hagberg hesitated.

He was no stranger to the country, having spent sixteen years with his wife, Nancy, as Baptist missionaries in Indonesian Borneo.

But that was nearly a quarter-century ago. He wondered if he was still up to the rigors of such a job. "I was thinking of all the reasons I shouldn't go, but I realized it was just something God wanted me to do," he said.

Today, the minister believes the experience changed his life.

From the depths of one of the worst natural disasters in recorded history, he found a bright, shining light. It was the light of a shared humanity that transcended cultural and religious differences.

Aceh, the territory where he volunteered, is a stronghold of fundamentalist Islam. It is also a hotbed of a long-running rebel insurgency against the Indonesian government. Before the tsunami hit, Aceh was largely a closed society, suspicious of outsiders.

Enter the bespectacled and soft-spoken Hagberg, who kept his Christian beliefs to himself, knowing he was there to help, not proselytize.

A conservative Baptist minister thrown together with fundamentalist Muslims in a ravaged and chaotic land? You might think this would be a recipe for a whole new level of seismic upheaval. But as Hagberg slogged through the mosquito-infested heat and humidity, he found just the opposite—something beyond beautiful, approaching the sublime.

New Friendships

He came expecting suspicion; he left having found that most elusive state of grace—brotherhood blind to race, creed, or nationality.

"They were just very kind, loving and affectionate," Hagberg said of the people whose lives he touched and who touched his. They were profoundly grateful to know an American traveled so far for no reason other than to hold out a helping hand.

"You really become part of each others lives in that situation," he reflected. "Talk about feeling a person's pain. You want to weep with them for their loss, you really do."

One man told him, "You are a member of my family. You are my brother."

A local leader, overwhelmed with gratitude, offered to build a house for Hagberg so he could return with his wife to live in the man's village. "That, I think, is the greatest compliment I've ever been given," Hagberg said.

He took some lessons home with him. He knows now that actions speak louder than words, and that empathy is a gift returned many times over. He learned that in matters of life and death, differences melt away.

Through the jungle of despair, he glimpsed an elusive path—the one that leads to peace on Earth.

John Paul Defined Essence of a Leader

Leadership.

Many attempt it; few succeed.

One who defined its very essence was the little Polish boy who grew up to be the shepherd of one billion Catholics.

For Pope John Paul II, leadership seemed to come naturally. It radiated off him, and he used it to not only steer his flock but influence presidents and dictators, kings and queens.

He had those special qualities that are so hard to define yet so obviously recognizable when you finally see them. He had them, just as the Reverend Dr. Martin Luther King Jr. had them. Just as Gandhi had them. And Mother Teresa and Churchill and FDR.

I was a college student when Karol Wojtyla ascended to the papacy in 1978, and for nearly three decades, I have struggled with my own relationship to him, disagreeing with many of his edicts—on the role of women in the church, on celibacy, homosexuality, artificial birth control, the use of condoms to prevent the spread of AIDS, and on and on—yet still finding myself in awe of this bigger-than-life man. Even as I disagreed, I respected the clarity of his convictions. I found myself liking him, just as I found myself liking Ronald Reagan, someone else with whom I found plenty to disagree.

This pope had a rare charisma, a quality William F. Buckley Jr. once described as "his special, penetrating, transcendent warmth."

That luminosity was hard to resist, winning over even that toughest crowd of all—teenagers. On his many trips around the globe, they flocked to him by the thousands. Parents could only marvel at the magic.

Traditional, old-school Catholics adored John Paul for many of the same reasons that disconcerted his critics. My parents were among his biggest fans. On a visit home after the pope's 1993 U.S. visit, I found an entire shelf lined with hand-labeled videotapes; Mom and Dad had recorded every single televised minute of his multi-day tour. Take that, Bruce Springsteen.

He was their rock star, their hero, their voice of conscience. More than anything, he was their rock, a voice of moral clarity in the wilderness.

And this perhaps will prove to be John Paul's greatest legacy. In a nuanced world of shades of gray, he rejected relativism and forcefully preached a vision of absolutes. He told Catholics what it meant to be Catholic, what was expected of them. You could agree or not—and often I did not—but there was no mistaking the message.

Many Catholics, adrift in the muddied turbulence that followed the church's Vatican II reforms of the 1960s, were grateful for the direction. Like a father who recognizes the need to give his children indisputable boundaries, Pope John Paul clearly set parameters that Catholics should live by. And, just as with children, the faithful found in those strictures stability and comfort.

He appeared guided by a moral authority so consistent, so strong and clear, even a nonbeliever could almost accept the Catholic proposition that he was a direct extension of the hand of God. His Holiness indeed seemed blessed with holiness. With goodness and decency.

When the pedophilia scandal swept the church, he seemed nearly as bereft and violated as the victims themselves. His anguish was palpable.

This pope was so many things: poet, athlete, academic, philosopher, multilingual intellectual, defender of innocence, crusher of communism, critic of capitalism, champion of the downtrodden. Mostly, he was an unstoppable force.

Shortly after becoming pope, he returned to his homeland and lent his legitimacy to a band of workers rising up in defiance of their communist overseers. The rest is history.

"He was a gift from the heavens to us," Lech Walesa, who founded the Solidarity movement in Poland, said last week.

If John Paul disdained communism, he also had plenty to say about the evils of Western affluence, its materialism and decadence. Even as he delighted conservatives, he hammered home issues dear to liberals' hearts—peace, nonviolence, economic justice. He forgave the man who tried to kill him. He reached out to Jews and Muslims. He decried the death penalty just as he decried abortion and euthanasia. He understood that if life is sacred, there can be no exceptions.

He chastised American presidents on more than one occasion, most recently President Bush's rush to war in Iraq. As one listened to him, it was clear he followed only one adviser, one opinion poll—his own moral code. If only all leaders could be so pure.

His was a remarkable life.

As word of his passing spread around the globe yesterday, I could not help thinking that even in death, the pope's leadership radiated. He showed the world how to accept the end of this life with dignity and grace.

It's Unhealthy, but It Is Legal

When I was ten, my best friend and I rode our bikes to the local bowling alley, slipped thirty-five cents into the vending machine, and bought our first pack of cigarettes.

In the woods nearby, we lit up—and promptly turned green. I decided then and there that if this was what it took to be cool, I'd gladly go through life as a dweeb.

To this day, I have little tolerance for cigarette smoke and even less for those inconsiderate slobs who think it is their God-given right to light up anytime, anyplace—and then toss their butts wherever they might fall.

I confess I'm annoyed by smokers in the workplace who spend ten minutes of every hour out in the parking lot puffing away on breaks their nonsmoking colleagues do not enjoy.

Basically, I hate everything about cigarettes. So why am I so uncomfortable with the growing national jihad against smokers?

It might have something to do with the fact that cigarette smoking is legal. Unhealthy, dangerous, stupid, but legal nonetheless.

And yet we increasingly treat cigarettes as contraband and those who indulge in them as social pariahs.

Cities are lining up to ban smoking in public gathering places, including bars and taverns, where smoking and drinking often go hand in hand. The Philadelphia City Council is set to vote Thursday on a widespread smoking prohibition. Mayor Street said he'd like to see a nationwide ban.

Workplace Litmus Test

And perhaps most troubling of all, Montgomery County is exploring a policy that would bar the hiring of smokers for county jobs.

We allegedly live in a free country, and that means having the freedom to indulge in harmful behavior. People smoke and drink too much and eat greasy burgers instead of salads and lounge in front of the television instead of exercise. And they will die younger because of it. Their choice.

Do we really want to go down this road of regulating legal but unhealthy behavior? If you want to take away my French fries, you'll have to pry them out of my cold, dead hand.

No one should be forced to breathe secondhand smoke, and smoking bans in workplaces, stores and government buildings make perfect sense.

But if a bunch of smokers want to sit in a smoke-filled bar and suck in one another's carbon monoxide over beer, shouldn't they have that right? I won't be there, but I respect their right to turn their lungs into tar pits.

Conversely, nonsmokers are free to choose smoke-free establishments to eat and drink. And the more they vote with their pocketbooks, the more clean-air joints will open.

Let the marketplace decide.

Freedom to Choose

A pub near my home went smoke-free last year, not because government put a gun to its head but because the owner saw money to be made. He lost the chain-smoking drinkers and gained the bigger-spending wine-and-dinner crowd.

When the place reeked of smoke, I chose to stay away; now I'm a regular. Isn't that how it should work?

Montgomery County thinks it can save on health care costs if it refuses to hire smokers. But wouldn't it make more sense to simply charge smoking employees a higher premium for health insurance? If they want to smoke, fine, but let them pay their way. If you have ever tried to buy life insurance, you know the stiff premiums smokers face. Fair enough.

What Montgomery County, or any employer, should really be concerned about is finding the best possible employee. Do you turn down a hard worker with a sterling resume and references because he smokes? Do you hire a nonsmoking slacker instead?

If cigarettes are really that harmful—and we all know they are—let's outlaw them. That might, after all, actually send an unmuddied message to our children about what we really think of these cancer sticks.

That, of course, will never happen, not so long as the tobacco industry has Congress eating out of its hand.

Before we start placing smokers in the public stocks, we might want to take a second look at that $10 billion (yes, billion) buyout Congress approved for tobacco growers last fall.

Isn't it all just a little hypocritical?

Shelter in Media Mocks Its Mission

Who said it's a dog's life?

For the dogs—and cats—at the Delaware County SPCA, life is anything but.

As the *Inquirer*'s Barbara Boyer has illustrated in a series of articles, the private, nonprofit animal shelter in Media makes a mockery of its name—the Society for the Prevention of Cruelty to Animals.

Does an organization dedicated to animals prevent cruelty by cramming dogs and cats into crowded, unsanitary conditions?

By allowing contagious diseases to run rampant through the facility? By blithely adopting desperately sick animals out to unsuspecting families who then face either mountainous veterinarian bills or the heartbreak of putting down the animal—or both?

Does it prevent cruelty by sitting on a $7.6 million nest egg while refusing to provide a modicum of veterinary care for its animals? By having a veterinarian on premises just two hours a week? Two hours for a facility that last year handled nearly three thousand dogs?

If this is where cruelty is prevented, I'd hate to see the torture chamber.

We humans expect certain minimum standards for our four-legged companions: safe, sanitary conditions, proper nutrition, clean drinking water, compassionate care, adequate medical attention.

It's not rocket science, and yet the shelter's thirteen-member board appears clueless on so many fronts, incapable of getting even the basics right.

Goodwill Gone Bad

The negligence is not malicious. It's benign in nature, good intentions overwhelmed by poor decisions—or no decisions at all.

Part of the problem seems to be the board's inability to wisely tap its $7.6 million endowment. Even conservatively invested with a 4 percent return, the investment would yield more than $300,000 a year in income; at a 6 percent return, the shelter has $456,000 a year to play with. Yet board members act like misers.

Nearly $8 million in the bank, and they can't afford $80,000 a year for a full-time veterinarian? Sorry, but that dog won't hunt.

"The board of directors just sits on the money," dog-rescue volunteer Arthur Herring 3rd of Montgomeryville told Boyer in frustration. "It's like a power trip for them."

Meanwhile, sick animals continue to go out to homes. Healthy animals continue to get infected. And the pathetic cycle continues.

Boyer has heard from people who adopted dogs and cats from the Delaware County shelter only to discover they were desperately ill. One woman took home a cat dying from the highly contagious feline HIV. Another adopted a German shepherd that spread a respiratory infection to the family's other dog. Yet another took home a pit bull mix, not knowing it was suffering from a highly contagious virus and internal bleeding. The dog required surgery, which cost the new owner $2,200.

Redefining "Humane"

A Collingdale woman took home a dog suffering from kennel cough, worms, and malnourishment. "I could count every rib on her body," the owner told Boyer.

That's what one might expect from a back-alley puppy mill, not from a well-meaning group with the words "prevention of cruelty" in its title.

Volunteers have quit in disgust. Visiting veterinarians have complained about the conditions. The state vows to investigate. And yet the board digs in its heels, stubbornly defending its incompetence and clinging to its miserable Typhoid Mary methods.

When one former SPCA board member, Joseph P. Boyle, pushed to improve conditions at the shelter, he was forced off the board. Boyle told the *Inquirer* that sick but treatable dogs were often euthanized because death was cheaper than medicine.

What is going on here?

Some animal advocates have begun a petition drive to recall all thirteen members of the shelter's board, and that is a good thing. Perhaps a complete change in leadership is what is needed to get this sorry excuse for an animal shelter back on track.

In the meantime, the existing board members need to tape reminders to their foreheads that read: "It's about preventing cruelty, stupid."

~~~~~

O'Reilly Doesn't Factor In the Truth

As far as lies go, this one was little.

In fact, upon reflection, it occurred to me that it might not be a lie at all but rather just a willful distortion based on a false assumption.

Either way, it told me something about the person behind it—Fox News blatherer-in-chief Bill O'Reilly.

O'Reilly has been criticized for manipulating facts to fit his agenda, most notably by political satirist Al Franken, who built an entire book, *Lies and the Lying Liars Who Tell Them*, around the premise.

As I read the book last year, I wondered whether Franken was exaggerating. Could this guy O'Reilly really play that fast and loose with the truth?

Then my little world collided with O'Reilly's by way of a dead Villanova professor named Mine Ener.

As the whole world now knows, Ener killed her Down syndrome baby and herself during postpartum psychotic episodes in 2003. Villanova created a firestorm last month when it erected a small plaque in its library to remember Ener for her contribution to the university before her descent into mental illness.

What was meant to be a simple statement of compassion was turned by talk radio, and later by O'Reilly, into an act of monstrous indecency—a Catholic institution honoring a baby-killer.

In a column Monday, I wondered aloud whether Jesus would be so quick to judge and condemn.

"Hiding Under His Desk"

On Monday, a Fox News producer in New York politely invited me to come on O'Reilly's show that night. I politely declined without giving a reason.

I thought that was the end of it. Then the taunting messages began.

Bill Hinski of Lansdale, who frequently grinds his teeth over my columns, gloated: "Missed you on *The O'Reilly Factor* last night. No guts?"

Another said: "Just was watching Bill O'Reilly. You can come out from under your desk now."

Huh?

I found a transcript of O'Reilly's show, and the mystery was solved. Sure enough, he had told his viewers that he had wanted to discuss the Villanova controversy with me, but "Mr. Grogan is hiding under his desk."

Gosh, I was?

As far as slams went, I had to admit it was pretty good: Liberal-leaning columnist needles conservative pundit in print, but runs scared when said pundit invites him to hash it out on his cable talk show. There was only one small problem. It was not true.

When *The O'Reilly Factor* aired at 8:00 P.M. Monday, I was not hiding under my desk. Wasn't even quivering in the broom closet. I was, in that same hour, appearing live on Philadelphia talk-radio station WPHT 1210 AM, which has led the charge to vilify Ener and Villanova University.

I appeared as a guest of host Dom Giordano, who easily is the most vitriolic brayer of them all on the topic. I had accepted Giordano's invitation before seeing O'Reilly's. Simple enough.

Lots of Company

Yet in O'Reilly's world, none of that mattered. It was of no concern that I was doing exactly what I would have been doing on his show, debating the topic in an antagonistic environment.

He did not bother to ask me why I declined his offer. All that counted was that I was a no-show. That made me a coward who lacked the courage of his convictions.

At least I was in good company.

I searched through Fox News transcripts from the last year and found that O'Reilly has accused others of the same thing, including the entire editorial hierarchy of the *New York Times* and the management of National Public Radio and Microsoft. He even accused the Terminator himself, Arnold Schwarzenegger, of hiding.

We were all quaking desk divers, lacking the mettle to confront the great and powerful Oz on his own turf.

Could it be that some people had better things to do? Or perhaps simply saw no value in trying to state their case in the shout-and-point quagmire of an O'Reilly slugfest?

Like I said, it's no big deal. Just a little lie based on a tiny assumption resulting in a minor distortion.

I think I'm gonna live.

But if my new friend Bill can play fast and loose with something as innocuous as a stranger's whereabouts, what else is he making up?

Zero Tolerance Running Amok

Today's question: How can we adults expect our children to respect us and our decisions when so often we act like total blockheads?

How can we ask them to accept our edicts without question when too often those edicts, however well-intentioned, are so wildly misguided?

Take zero-tolerance policies in our schools. They are in place for a reason. Weapons and drugs have no place in schools. But the words zero and tolerance, when combined, add up to one scary concept: blind enforcement with no room for common sense.

And when that happens, what are we left with? Injustice. And kids who lose faith and grow jaded. No wonder they look at us like we were just beamed down from Planet Clueless.

Exhibit A: The case of the crampy honors student.

As reported by Stephanie L. Arnold in Saturday's *Inquirer*, a senior on the honor roll at Haverford High School had the temerity to take an over-the-counter pain medication—a generic version of Aleve—for menstrual cramps without first clearing it with the school nurse.

Mind you, she is eighteen, old enough to fight and die in Iraq. Mind you, she was not misusing the pain medicine. Mind you, she made no attempt to hide her behavior. In fact, she was busted after she went to the nurse and reported that her cramping continued, despite the pill she took.

A World Without Grays

Does this sound like a crazed drug abuser to you? In the black-and-white world of zero tolerance, the question is moot. She violated the school's drug policy, which bans students from, among other things, taking medication without permission. And she was suspended, if only for part of one day before she apologized and was allowed back in school.

The girl's mother about nailed it when she likened the policy to "throwing a hand grenade on an anthill."

Unfortunately, the problem is not isolated, which leads to Exhibit B: The case of the handcuffed ten-year-old.

Porsche Brown, a fourth grader at Holme Elementary School in Northeast Philadelphia, was suspended after an eight-inch pair of scissors was found in her book bag. But the saga did not end there. Police arrived, handcuffed the pint-size fugitive, and carted her down to the local precinct house in the back of a police wagon.

Geez, I'd hate to see what they would have done had she been packing a stapler and Elmer's glue.

It's more than a little ridiculous. It's plain dumb. Everyone agrees the child meant no harm in bringing the scissors to school. Yet, at the time, the police policy was to cuff all weapons suspects, regardless of age. And so a child was treated like a criminal.

Schools chief Paul Vallas and city Police Commissioner Sylvester Johnson later apologized to the girl's mother, admitting the principal and cops overreacted. Ya think?

A Syrup-Crusted Blade

And, finally, consider Exhibit C: The case of the sticky eating utensil.

This one involves yet another honors student, Peter De-Witt, a senior at Great Valley High School in Chester County. DeWitt's car was singled out for a drug search in the school's parking lot in September. No drugs were found, but authorities did spot a small penknife and a steak knife.

DeWitt explained that he used the penknife to tinker with his car stereo. The steak knife had been used by his sister, who ate a plate of waffles in the car on the way to school with him. The parents—who, by supplying the waffles, I suppose were accessories to the crime—confirmed his story.

The alleged weapons never even left the confines of the locked car. Harmless enough, you say? Sorry, no room for reason. Under zero tolerance, DeWitt faced possible expulsion until cooler heads prevailed three days into his suspension.

In each of these cases lurks a glimmer of justification. Children can and do harm themselves by improperly taking medications. Children can and do use something as innocuous as scissors or a utensil to harm others.

There should be no room in schools for harmful behavior of any type. But there should be room for common sense, discretion, and intelligence.

If we want our kids to respect authority, we owe them that much.

Two Pieces of Tin Open Flood of Memories

Richard Hiebsch said goodbye to Vietnam thirty-five years ago. Or so he thought.

After two tours of duty as an infantryman, he returned home to Philadelphia, landed a job as a railroad conductor, got married, reared two kids.

Years passed, and then decades. The searing images of combat faded.

Then, on November 14—"the Sunday after Veterans Day" is how he remembers it—came the phone call.

Hiebsch and his wife, Barbara, returned to their home in Norristown to find a message waiting on their answering machine. A woman's voice.

"She said, 'Are you Richard Hiebsch? I think I have something of yours that you left in Vietnam,'" he recalled.

A flood of long-buried emotions rose in his throat. His heart pounding, Hiebsch, fifty-six, called back. That's when he met Stacey Hansen, thirty-six, a firefighter in San Jose, California, who has made two trips to Vietnam.

On her most recent visit in September, she was in the city of Hue and stopped to buy water from a roadside vendor. The old man had a small table covered with trinkets. In a glass bowl, something caught her eye.

"There was a set of dog tags," Hiebsch said. "She picked them up and saw they were American. They were mine. I think she paid $2 for them."

A Note of Thanks

A week later, a package arrived. Inside, there they were, two stamped pieces of metal bearing his name, serial number, blood type, religious preference. Hansen had included a note: "I want to say thank you for your service and all that you sacrificed over there. I'm so sorry for the way you guys were treated when you came home. I'll never understand it."

As it turns out, Hansen has made it her mission to reunite lost tags with their owners. In her two trips, she has bought more than two thousand American dog tags being sold on the streets as souvenirs. So far, she and her partner, Bryan Marks, a fellow firefighter, have returned more than four hundred of them (www.vietnamdogtags.com). They accept no money in return.

For Hiebsch, the moment he opened the box was the moment he allowed a large and defining part of his life back in, as well.

"In that second, I remembered everything," Hiebsch said. "It completely took me back."

Where it took him was to Quang Tri Province and the 1968 Tet Offensive.

Hiebsch was twenty, just eighteen months out of Cardinal Dougherty High. He was a foot soldier, a grunt, loaded down with ammo cases, spare radio batteries, machine-gun belts, two mortar rounds—some sixty pounds in all.

"I was standing in line waiting to get in the chopper, and I looked down and all of a sudden I have no dog tags. They weren't there."

Later, he was issued a new set. "That was the end of it," he said.

Today he is glad to have them back. Beyond glad, really, for these two corroded pieces of tin connect him viscerally to a past he had tried to erase.

Like Fresh Air

"Everything was so negative all these years, and you try to put it out of your head," he said. "Then all of a sudden out of the blue comes this little thing, and it's like fresh air in a stagnant room. I don't know how to explain it. It just kind of over-whelms you that way."

Receiving his lost dog tags has allowed him to confront the pain he had buried.

"We had as much courage as any soldier who ever put on a uniform," he said. "We fought as hard as any. We did an admirable job. We won every battle but lost the war. I don't want any soldier to ever have to go through the negativity that we did."

He polished his tags with a toothbrush and framed them on a bed of black velvet, displayed in his den.

At the VFW hall in Gladwyne, he said, the tags have made quite a stir. Other veterans, many of them from the last great war, the one that ended with parades and ticker tape, pepper him with questions.

"When I saw the World War II guys flock around me, I felt honored," Hiebsch said. "This was the generation that saved our generation."

Honored and deeply grateful to a woman he has never met. "That she could do this and not know anybody who she's doing it for, it's amazing," he said.

"I guess that's the American spirit."

Treasured Times—and Regrets

It seems many of us have made that last trip home.

After writing about my own visit to my dying father, I heard from dozens who had made that same difficult but essential journey to say goodbye, and from dozens of others who know they will be making it soon. I also heard from those who missed their chance, who delayed too long, and even now, years later, deeply regret it.

There will be no last names in this column because many of the responses I received were intensely personal.

Wrote Roger: "I still feel guilty about not having said my goodbyes to my father before his death to tell him one last time how much he meant to me."

And from Robert: "I was fortunate that the last thing I ever said to my dad was 'I love you.' For you to have gotten that gift is the best."

. Anita was at her job in Center City when the call came from the nursing home that her mother had taken a turn. The daughter arrived at her mother's bedside twenty minutes before her death. "I was with her, holding her hand, and praying every prayer I ever knew into her ear," she wrote.

John spent Thanksgiving seven years ago with his father, walking on the beach and talking. "Two days later I received a call that my dad dropped dead while putting on his slippers. He was sixty-six, fit, and in perfect health. So I tell people to make their connections now because you just never know."

A Peaceful Time

Added Gail, who moved her dying mother back home to Phoenixville from Florida: "I am so grateful that I was able to have her with me for her final days."

It took Kevin forty-eight years and the death of his mother to realize something: "You see, 'real men do cry,' and they do say 'I love you.'"

James in Doylestown makes a point to have lunch with his eighty-six-year-old mother every day, not knowing which might be the last. "It is hard to say goodbye and to say how much you love your parents," he wrote, "but better to say it than to leave it unsaid."

Paul made that trip two years ago. "It was difficult, [but] the memories from my last few days with Dad are nothing short of priceless."

"I lost my father very suddenly, almost ten years ago, when he was only sixty," wrote Mary Fran. "What I wouldn't have given to have had a chance for one last meaningful visit."

Likewise, Mike's father left for his job at Conrail twenty-three years ago and never returned—struck and killed by a train. "I would give anything to have one more day with him," he said.

Debbie looks at her aging parents "and I realize my time with them is nearing an end. As an only child who hasn't married, I see that our branch of the family tree is about to fall off."

Missed Opportunities

Victor's regrets have spanned the last half-century: "Fresh out of college and caught up in the demands of a new career, I never said those heartfelt words to my father in the late 1950s even though I knew that his heart disease would soon claim his life."

More regrets from Angelo: "My dad taught my brother and me that true men never told another man they loved him. I am sorry now that I never spoke that word to my dad. He never told us he loved us, either. I guess he thought we knew."

If there is a consensus here, it is to not delay. Procrastinate on your taxes, on paying the phone bill—but not on telling your aging parents what is in your heart.

I made my trek to the house I grew up in near Detroit over Thanksgiving. Two weeks later, my father was back in the hospital, and a few days after that in the intensive care unit, his breathing aided by a heavy plastic mask that made talking nearly impossible.

He died two days before Christmas, all four of his children beside him, a soft snow falling outside his window as if a gift sent from heaven.

I don't need to say how treasured those last few days together, while my father was still at home and his old self, have already become. Treasured beyond words. Instead, I will leave you with Lisa, whose eighty-three-year-old father died unexpectedly of a stroke, not allowing time for goodbyes.

"I guess what I'm getting at is that time is precious," she wrote. "Always let them know what you are feeling. Never wait."

The Hardest Trip Worth Taking

Some trips home are harder than others. This one was the hardest of all.

Home for me is the house I grew up in near Detroit, the house where my parents still live, although for how much longer not even they can say.

At eighty-eight, my mother is frail and forgetful but, with her new hip and heart bypass, otherwise going strong.

It's my father. Until two months ago, he was always the robust one, physically strong, mentally sharp, of near boundless energy. He doted over his bride, cut his own acre of grass, climbed ladders, shoveled snow, attended daily Mass.

Then came the diagnosis of leukemia followed by the precipitous drops in his blood counts and the poison that masquerades as medicine.

My father did not want me to come. "You have your own family now," he protested. I showed up anyway. Disobeying never felt more right.

My father was home from the hospital, if only temporarily, and the full, devastating effects of the chemotherapy had not yet arrived. He was weak but comfortable, his mind clear.

He was turning eighty-nine.

This was our window to be together. Neither of us would say it, but we both knew the window was closing.

We sat at the kitchen table and talked. Just talked—about health and grandkids and home repairs. When he grew tired, I went outside to rake leaves and put up storm windows. When I returned, the house was as quiet as a shrine, and I walked from room to room with my memories.

The once-blazing, now-cold fireplace. The long-silent piano. The kitchen sink that will always be synonymous with my mother. In the basement, I stood at the workbench where Dad had taught me to drive a nail.

When he awoke, he asked me to bring him the wooden box I had made for him from hardwoods I had harvested from the woods behind my house. He opened the lid and one by one pulled out his most precious keepsakes.

There was the gold watch his father had received from the Rapid Motor Company for being on the first motorcar to ascend Pikes Peak, Colorado.

There was his school ring, University of Michigan, Class of '39. His World War II navy bars; his service pins from a career at General Motors, their tiny diamond chips shimmering. And his most treasured possession of all: his grandfather's silver rosary.

He described each one, and when he was done, he laid the objects back into the box and closed the lid.

"How does meatloaf sound tonight?" I asked. "It's my specialty."

"Meatloaf sounds good," he said.

After the dinner dishes were cleared, I summoned my nerve and asked my father for a favor: Would he mind letting me interview him about his life? I dreaded asking because everyone knows children do not ask for such things until time is running out.

He cheerfully agreed, and for the next two hours he talked and I listened as the video camera captured for my children and theirs to come the stories of his life. His childhood growing up in Germantown, swimming in the Wissahickon Creek. His military service. Parenthood.

Even as he spoke, I knew he was giving me the greatest gift possible.

The next morning we were all up before the sun, even Mom, who these days sleeps late. A flight waited to return me to my other life, the life of husband, father, and wage earner.

As sons always must, I had to leave.

The Grogan men have never been demonstrative with their feelings. Growing up, my father and I would greet each other not with a kiss or hug but with a handshake. We followed the rule that the L-word was better shown than spoken.

But on this morning, standing in the garage, his cane dangling from his wrist, he held out his arms to me.

"Dad," I said, summoning the words I had said so seldom. "I love you."

He responded so quickly, so automatically, the words rushing out, that it was as if he had been waiting all these years for permission to speak.

"I love you, too, Johnny," he said.

Johnny. He had not called me that since I was a little boy. Johnny.

On the drive to the airport, I realized something. Something big: There are hard trips home, but no wasted ones.

Earth Versus the Mall People

A government spy satellite roaming the Milky Way in search of extraterrestrial life has picked up a transmission coming from an unknown planet.

Buzzzzzzzz. Schplunkt!

"Commander, I have just returned from my reconnaissance trip to the planet Earth."

"Ah, very good, Cygot. And what did you find there?"

"It is a strange and incomprehensible place. I landed in a confederacy of united but deeply divided states, some red, some blue. There was a place called Joisey, where the people speak a monosyllabic guttural dialect. And a place named Philly where the local language is even harder to decipher. But the oddest findings came in the countryside, in a vast sprawling kingdom called Suburbia."

"What did you see in this Suburbia?"

"I saw heavily armed men dress in orange and head out into the woods where they blasted away at anything that moved, sometimes hitting each other, sometimes hitting four-legged life forms. And yet at the end of each day they returned to eat an odd energy roll known as 'cheesesteak.'"

"Strange indeed."

"And that's just the beginning, commander. I arrived on a day called Thanksgiving, a tribal holiday to count blessings."

"And how do they mark this sacred day?"

"By eating vast quantities of food, sir. Some even unbutton their pants."

"And then what do they do with all this energy they have consumed?"

"They sleep, sir."

A Predawn Sojourn

"A sort of hibernation?"

"Not exactly. The feast appears to be the start of a vast national marathon they call 'Just Twenty-nine Shopping Days to Christmas.' Within hours they are up again, and they head off in darkness to giant edifices surrounded by acres of a gray stone-like surface."

"Their sacred temples, no doubt."

"Yes, and they call these temples all the same name: Mall. The worshipers wait for hours to get inside the doors."

"And what do they do once inside?"

"They use small plastic cards to spend riches they do not have for goods they do not need."

"Goods they do not need?"

"Such as clear stones the slave class digs from the earth."

"They pay vast sums for mere stones?"

"The males hand them to the females who then agree to bear their progeny."

"A fertility rite! And what else?"

"The females wear ceremonial gold and buy expensive pouches to hold their plastic cards. They buy paint for their faces and many pairs of leather coverings for their feet."

"Why many pairs when they have but one pair of feet?"

"Inexplicable, commander, but their closets overflow with them. And the men fill their garages with the lumbering personal transporters known as SUVs, which suck finite fossil fuels from the ground and force the nations to battle each other."

Zombie Nation

"And who commands them to buy these useless things?"

"The orders come from the Great Persuaders, who rule from a place called Madison Avenue. They decide what the masses must buy and send messages through the electronic tubes in every dwelling, telling the people they are nothing without these items."

"And the people fall for this?"

"No questions asked, sir. Especially during the Christmas twenty-nine-day marathon."

"And how is this race won?"

"It seems the household with the most items on Christmas Day is the winner."

"And how do they celebrate?"

"I am told they will awaken before dawn the day after and return to the mall temples, where they will exchange the many things they acquired during the marathon for yet more possessions."

"And they do this to celebrate this day they call Christmas?"

"They call it a religious holiday."

"And what is this day? Surely, it must stand for more than that which the plastic card can obtain."

"It once did, I am told, commander. But the people became blinded at the mall temples, and the original meaning appears to have been lost long ago."

"Cygot, your excellent surveillance disturbs me greatly. Now to the decontamination unit before the Earthling consumption disease gets loose."

Instead of Chintz, She Got Chintzy

Oh what a difference two little digits can make.

Justina Clark, an eighty-year-old widow, learned that lesson with ear-popping, cheek-blushing clarity this week when she got a hankering for upholstery fabric and picked up the telephone.

Clark was watching a favorite soap opera on KYW-TV (Channel 3) in her cozy North Philadelphia row house Tuesday when a commercial came on for Hancock Fabrics, a national chain with outlets in Pennsylvania. For months Clark had been thinking of re-covering a threadbare chair in her dining room,

and the commercial, with its promise of great selection at com-
petitive prices, caught her attention. She jotted down the toll-
free number on the screen.

But when she dialed, she received quite a surprise. Instead of
a knowledgeable fabric clerk, she was greeted by a young
woman's come-hither voice making an unabashed come-on to
male suitors. "Hurry, I'm waiting," the voice cooed.

Clark had dialed in search of chintz and landed square in the
middle of a phone-sex operation.

"This lady was being very explicit," said Clark, who worked
for thirty-two years as a personnel assistant at the old Philadelphia Naval Shipyard. "It's the first time I've ever heard anything like that. When she got to the part about 'spread-eagle,'
I hung up."

Oh my.

Figuring she had mis-dialed, Clark double-checked the
number she had written down and tried again, but reached the
same sleazy recording.

A Call to Duty

Her next call was to KYW, where she was unable to reach
anyone who knew about the advertisement. Then she called
me. I, of course, volunteered to jump right on the case.

I dialed the toll-free number. Sure enough, I was greeted by
the purr of a cartoonishly over-the-top sex kitten. Think Mar-
ilyn Monroe meets Jessica Rabbit. The recording promised me
anything "your nastiest imagination can dream up," adding:
"After all, it is your fantasy, and we live to make it real."

Gee, and I just wanted a bolt of taffeta.

Marilyn/Jessica teased, "Me and my ultra-hot girlfriends will
do whatever it takes . . ."

Me and my ultra-hot girlfriends? My mind flashed back to Mrs. Anderson, my eighth-grade English teacher. "I believe you meant to say, 'My ultra-hot girlfriends and I,'" I offered helpfully.

Just then, she asked for my credit-card number. The honeymoon was over. Dang, and I thought she really liked me.

I finally got through to a real live woman named Kelly in customer service who confirmed that: (1) She received a fair number of wrong numbers from shocked elderly women; (2) they "usually are pretty upset about it"; and (3) this thriving phone-sex service operates right here in our own City of Brotherly Love. And who said all the quality jobs were moving to India?

Eyes Playing Tricks

My next call was to Hancock Fabrics' corporate office outside Tupelo, Mississippi, where I broke the bad news of the phone mix-up to a nice woman named Brenda.

"Oh no!" she said.

Brenda connected me to James Gilmore, Hancock's advertising director. "Our number is 877-HANCOCK, and that is the number that has appeared on the bottom of every ad we've ever run on TV," he said. "Your readers have misread it; they see a toll-free number and they automatically assume it's 800."

He said the company had tried to obtain the 800 number about five years ago, but it was already taken—at the time he didn't know by whom—and so Hancock settled for the less familiar toll-free 877 exchange. He estimated that one of a hundred callers made the same mistake Clark had.

"We've had this complaint over the years. They see 877 but dial 800, and when they do, they're truly mortified," he said.

When I called Clark to tell her she must have misread the number, she already had figured out her error. A friend who videotapes the same soap opera watched the tape, and confirmed that the number on the screen, sure enough, had an 877 prefix.

"When I hear 'toll-free,' I think '1-800,'" Clark said. An easy mistake to make—and one the blushing widow vowed never to make again.

~~~

Twist of Fate Aids the Pretzel Man

The MacDade Crossing shopping plaza is ordinary in every way. There is a pharmacy, a fitness center, an ice cream parlor.

Then you spot the man in the wheelchair selling pretzels.

His name is John Magowan, and he sits behind a flimsy table on the sidewalk at this plaza in Ridley Township on a brisk afternoon, eking out what living he can.

The Pretzel Man has his regulars, and they all greet him by name as they press a buck or two into his hand. No one asks for change. Some don't even bother taking a pretzel.

"I've been a pretzel man for thirty-five years now," Magowan, who lives in subsidized housing in Woodlyn, tells you. "I've been at this spot for eighteen years. You get to know a lot of people over that time."

One customer asks, "John, you doing all right today?"

"I'm hanging in there," the Pretzel Man answers stoically.

For Magowan, fifty-five, who has been using a wheelchair since he was a toddler, hanging in there is about as good as life serves up.

Born with cerebral palsy, he has never walked more than a few yards, despite numerous operations on his useless legs. He now suffers a host of ancillary problems, including diabetes, degenerative joint disease, and chronic bladder infections. "It's what you call a lifetime disease," he says.

No Time for Self-Pity

His father, Chuck Magowan, a retired minister in South Philadelphia, later will explain: "He could have gone into a corner and never come out, but he didn't do that. He makes his own way in the world. He doesn't feel sorry for himself."

Despite the cards life has dealt him, the Pretzel Man says he feels like the luckiest soul on earth these days. Well, perhaps not the luckiest—his broken body is never lost on him—but fortunate nonetheless.

His wife of twenty-eight years, Debbie, pulls to the curb in a gleaming, if not quite new, minivan equipped with a wheelchair lift. And you see in his eyes why he feels so blessed.

For years, the van was an out-of-reach dream, essential to his independence yet far beyond his means. Instead, Debbie Magowan drove her husband to the plaza on MacDade Boulevard to sell pretzels each day in a cramped Dodge Neon. A tiny woman who suffers osteoporosis, she had to help him out of his wheelchair and into the car by lifting him by the seat of his pants. "It was hard on both our backs," she says.

Increasingly, the task was becoming too much for her. The Pretzel Man could see his fragile freedom in the crosshairs.

And so several months ago, the couple began trying to raise donations for a custom lift van, which costs upwards of $45,000. But despite publicity in a local newspaper, the account topped out at $325.

The dream, it appeared, was dead.

A Guardian Angel

And that is when the man Magowan now calls his "guardian angel" came into his life.

George Hess, a retired Amtrak electrician from Folsom, had known Magowan and his parents years ago through a church they attended in Aston. When he read in the *Delaware County Daily Times* about Magowan's need for the special van, he knew what he had to do.

The eighty-six-year-old widower raided his retirement nest egg and handed the Magowans $20,000. "I was as tickled about it as he was," he said. "I was just glad to be able to help John out."

From there, Rothrock Chevrolet in Springfield hunted down a 1996 Dodge Grand Caravan equipped with a lift that came in just under $20,000.

The Pretzel Man at long last had his ride. And with it the continued promise of an independent life.

"It's like a dream come true," Magowan says.

Debbie walks to the van and proudly shows off how the doors open, how the lift works. Instead of a front passenger seat, the van has a spot to lock a wheelchair in place so her husband can ride beside her. Come Thanksgiving, she says, the couple will have much for which to be grateful.

"There are still a bunch of nice people in the world," she says. "At times it doesn't seem like it, but there are."

Up in the Treetops Sits Old, Slow Dad

The aerial office is now officially open for business. And just in time for the coming of fall colors.

As the name implies, my new office is perched eighteen feet in the air in the woods behind my house, swaying in the tree-tops. It hangs in defiance of gravity between a birch and a sassafras tree, suspended by a Rube Goldberg–style contraption of my own making that I swear is as solid as the Betsy Ross Bridge, even as it creaks and groans in the slightest breeze.

The furnishings are spare to the point of Spartan: a bean bag to sit on; a low folding table on which to rest a mug of coffee; a throw rug over the plywood floor. I've dragged up a couple of milk cartons to serve as bookcases.

The aerial office has a green metal roof and three windows, with lovely views into the treetops. It has a cantilevered deck that begs to be spit off, and a bucket on a rope that allows me to hoist emergency rations between trips back to terra firma.

The aerial office was not always so employed. Until just a few weeks ago, it was a children's tree fort, designed and built for kids at the urging of kids—three kids in particular, all of whom share my last name.

They wanted a tree fort. Wanted one more than anything in this world. Wanted it please-please-please-Dad bad. How can a father say no to that? So the old man got busy.

Deceptive Advertising

I'm still miffed at Home Depot for a television advertisement I consider wildly misleading. In it, a clueless dad just like me walks into the store saying his kid wants a tree fort. Within seconds, the helpful employee has him all loaded up, and by commercial's end, the happy father and son are camped out in the completed structure, which looks just slightly less ornate than Monticello.

Let's just say when I showed up in need at Home Depot, it took me a half-hour to find someone to talk to and another half-hour to figure out how to pull the lumber off the shelves without triggering an avalanche.

I can't blame it all on the store. My problem is that my skills as a carpenter are roughly equal to my skills as a speaker of ancient Greek. The learning curve was something fierce, and the work plodded ahead at a pace most often associated with large, continent-sized blocks of ice.

Working on any building project would be a long, slow slog for me, but working six yards up in the air while teetering atop a wobbly ladder slowed me beyond glacial, to the pace of a PennDot road crew.

Did I mention my lifelong aversion to heights? Eighteen feet does not sound like much until you are swaying in the wind, trying to swing a hammer with nothing but air between you and the hard, rocky ground. Then you might as well be hanging over the Grand Canyon. Either way, one false move and you're toast.

A Snail's Pace

Start to finish, the project took me more than a year. Go ahead, home-improvement guys, laugh into your tool belts. Pathetic, I know.

My wife observed that most men would have been able to complete, say, the Hoover Dam in the time it took me to build my children's five-by-seven-foot tree hut. She always exaggerates. Maybe a public library, but not the Hoover Dam.

This is all to say that by the time I had the floor joists strung, the walls up, and the roof on, the kids had long since moved on to the next fantasy.

"Hey, Dad," the middle one said when I came in from a particularly grueling white-knuckle workday up in the swaying trees. "Will you make us a go-cart? Oh, please, please, please? We could take apart the lawn mower."

"Give me strength," I said. That's when I realized I had two choices: Abandon my floating Taj Mahal to the squirrels, or move in myself.

Which is what I did over the weekend. Not to sleep or eat, just to sit and think and gaze and dream far from the cacophony of my everyday life.

In the aerial office, there are no phones, no radios, no televisions, no beeping e-mails. There are only trees and sky and falling leaves. And the chatter of the occasional blue jay.

Life seems clearer up there. Life's simple, small joys clearer still.

As for the go-cart, the kids will just have to ask their mom.

Don't Tell Her Not to Play the Slots

In an earlier, better time, Patricia McNally enjoyed horseback riding, tennis, and badminton. She loved to dance. "Sex was good, too," she says with a wry laugh, "but, oh well."

Now, at age sixty-nine, the West Chester grandmother is racked by degenerative arthritis that has turned her bones brittle and forced her to undergo two spinal fusions and several other surgeries. She is in near constant pain and has had to abandon all her physical hobbies.

These days, McNally has found a comforting substitute for the joy her active lifestyle once gave her—playing the slot machines.

She does not agree with those who believe slots gambling is a troubling and exploitative business that in effect taxes the poor, the elderly, and the unsophisticated. She fully understands that slot machines offer astronomically bad odds of winning and that they are designed to string players along, draining their wallets.

That does not stop her from feeding in quarters. To her, slot machines are just one thing: a splash of escapist fun on an otherwise bleak canvas.

"When you get to be my age, there's not a lot of excitement," she says. "Quite frankly, playing the slots is crazy. The percentages are stacked against you. But it has an element of excitement you can't get anywhere else, at least not at our age. The fireworks, you've got to get them where you can find them."

A Disciplined Approach

And so a few times a year, she and her husband of thirty-eight years, Jim, journey out of state to gamble, sometimes no farther away than Delaware Park near Wilmington, other times to Las Vegas or Lake Tahoe. She welcomes legalized slots gambling in Pennsylvania, even though the couple plan to move to Arizona later this year. After all, she figures, Pennsylvanians such as her will continue to gamble; the state might as well reap the tax benefits.

A former trust officer for a bank in West Chester, McNally never gambled until after she retired. She is typical of many of the players in slots parlors where, on any given day, retired, white-haired women can be found in disproportionate numbers.

McNally bristles at the characterization of those on fixed incomes blowing their Social Security checks in the casinos. She and her husband live on comfortable pensions and set limits each day they gamble. Hers is $100, and when the money is gone, she is done. She recognizes that not all slots players exercise such discipline and that many gamblers end up enslaved to the rush of the machines. But as she says, "Addiction is a personal problem not directly related to slots. I know people who are addicted to exercise."

Even on losing days, she considers it $100 well spent, just as she would if she spent $100 for a theater ticket and dinner out. The difference, she says, is that a day at the slots holds the promise, however remote, of a payback. And a thrill.

Lucky Moments

On some days luck is with her. Her biggest haul came in Nevada last year. She pumped $20 into a dollar slot machine and hit the $800 jackpot. Another time, on a cruise ship, she was down to her last four quarters when some $400 in tokens rained down.

"When I'm in the casino and hear that ka-ching, ka-ching, somehow my pain goes away," she says.

McNally knows slots gambling could bring to Pennsylvania a host of social problems, from addiction to bankruptcy to family discord. But she wants the world to know that not every slots player is poor and desperate and hoping against hope to win back the rent money.

Some, like her, are simply old and achy and hungry for a glimmer of the spark they once knew life could hold.

"If you can't dance anymore, and you can't ride horses, and you can't play golf and you can't play tennis . . . " she says, not finishing the sentence. "One by one, these things get taken away from you. You can sit and sulk or you can substitute with something else."

And then she adds, without a trace of self-pity: "Inside all of us is that little desire for excitement, even when everything else is gone."

A Lonely Death, a Forgotten Life

As the country paused to bid farewell to a beloved former president Friday, I found myself paying my last respects to another fallen American, this one unknown and unmissed, her passing unmarked.

I found her fresh grave in a mowed field just off Interstate 78 in Lehigh County, a few miles west of Allentown. In one direction loomed a concrete plant; in the other the soaring roller coasters of Dorney Park and Wildwater Kingdom.

I parked my car and walked to the grave, a heap of wet, red clay still piled high atop it. A small laminated printout on a metal stake passed for a gravestone. It read: "Jane Doe, May 12, 2004, County of Lehigh."

For this American, there would be no horse-drawn caisson, no jet flyovers, no solemn speeches or foreign dignitaries. There would be no tears, not even a name.

She was believed to be homeless, and she was crushed by a van as it backed into a parking space in Allentown on April 29. The woman lingered unconscious in a hospital for nearly two weeks.

Her pockets were empty except for a bottle of lice shampoo and an envelope containing $269 cash. She carried no identification, and no one reported her missing. When police officers canvassed the area, no one remembered her. Her fingerprints were untraceable.

It was almost as if Jane Doe had never existed.

A Few Sketchy Facts

Before I visited the grave, Paul Zondlo, Lehigh County's chief deputy coroner, who accumulated a five-hundred-page file attempting to identify the woman, told me everything that is known about her.

"White female, probably in her early sixties to early seventies," he said. "She was a small woman, about five foot three to five foot seven, 100 to 110 pounds. No distinguishing characteristics. She was wearing a blue ski-type jacket and white suede shoes. She had mid-length gray hair with darker roots. Basically, that's about it."

One oddity about Jane Doe was what hospital workers found when she arrived. Over her hair she was wearing a lice-infested dark curly wig. It had been on her head so long, Zondlo said, that her hair had grown through the wig's netting, requiring hospital workers to cut it off her.

"We put her picture in the newspaper," Zondlo said. "Usually when we put a description in the newspaper, within hours we have people who call in with information, and most of the time the information is good."

But not this time.

"This kind of gives you a kick in the gut," he said. "We've never had this before. We've never had one we couldn't identify."

On Tuesday, Jane Doe was placed in a pressboard box and buried without ceremony in the county's cemetery for indigents, at the end of a long row of unadorned graves. "This one is sad," Zondlo said. "She's buried now, and her family doesn't even know—if indeed she had a family."

Questions Remain

Who was this woman? We probably will never know, although the coroner's office has preserved samples of her DNA in case new leads come in.

What brought her to be huddled alone wearing an old wig at the back of a parking space? In this great land of opportunity, in this country that prides itself on its safety nets for the elderly, how did this come to be? She was somebody's daughter, and perhaps somebody's mother, as well.

In America, all men are created equal. But we do not all grow up equal. And we do not all live equal. And in the end we do not all die equal. Last week, more than most weeks, in a muddy potter's field by the side of a busy highway, that hard truth was self-evident. One America, two worlds. One people indivisible, two lives. And two very different deaths.

As millions watched President Reagan being eulogized at the National Cathedral, I stood alone beneath a leaden sky with the forgotten remains of another American. The roar of passing truck traffic provided a sort of melancholy funeral dirge.

Rest in peace, Jane Doe, whoever you were, wherever you came from, whatever the eclipsed arc of your American dream.

War Comes Home to West Chester

With its comfortable colonial homes and green carpets of lawn, Estate Drive in West Whiteland Township near here hardly looks like the latest front of the war in Iraq. But that is what it has become.

The war came home to Pennsylvania in a powerful and disturbing way this week. It came from halfway around the globe and landed like a percussion bomb in this tree-lined neighborhood where the rumble of lawn mowers had been one of the few distractions to suburban serenity.

As the whole world now knows, the war came to the home of Michael and Suzanne Berg, whose twenty-six-year-old son was executed in Iraq by masked terrorists seeking to avenge the humiliation and mistreatment of Iraqi detainees at Abu Ghraib prison.

Nick Berg, Henderson High School Class of '96, was in Iraq not as a soldier or prison guard or interrogator. He did not humiliate or abuse anyone.

He was in Iraq, his family said, to find work in his specialty of servicing telecommunications towers. As the United States Commerce Department is quick to point out, Iraq is the next big business opportunity waiting to happen. Berg was chasing that dream.

And now he is dead, beheaded as video cameras rolled. And the only question left for us to answer as we reel with revulsion at the utter barbarity of this crime, is how we as a community will respond.

An Eye for an Eye?

Will we demand our own vengeance for theirs? Will we cheer, or perhaps just quietly nod, at the deaths of more Iraqi civilians? Will we want to, as I heard one man propose, "carpet-bomb the whole damn country"?

Or will we somehow find it in us to rise above the hate and antipathy and prove we are better than that?

Yesterday, a few doors from the Berg home, I found Kathy McCauley in her yard, watching her three young children. The questions were on her mind, too.

As a mother, she can only imagine the Bergs' anguish. As a neighbor, she offers her prayers and support. As an American, she has deep misgivings.

An American battalion commander in Baghdad this week attributed some of the abuse of Iraqi prisoners to a soldier who sought to avenge the rape of prisoner of war Jessica Lynch. Berg's killers, in turn, sought to avenge the prison abuse. Iraqis hang the charred remains of American contractors from a bridge. American soldiers respond in force.

McCauley has watched the spiraling brutality and inhumanity of war. She has seen the depraved photos. She has tried to explain to her family the reasons for this war, which has arrived on her street to claim a young man who once took the same school bus her children now take.

And she asked: "Where has our human race gone to? Where is it all going to end?" Squinting into the sun, she added, "I don't have an answer to that." None of us does.

A Downward Cycle

It has become a well-worn cliché, yet one that on this day, on this street, in a house where a devastated family huddles in grief, bears repeating: Violence breeds violence. Inhumanity begets inhumanity. Incivility spreads like an infectious disease.

You're disgusted and angry; I am, too. But you know how we win in the end? How we win not just the battle that is Iraq but the broader, much tougher war to convince Arabs worldwide that we act with noble intentions?

We win by showing the world that Americans are better than this. That Americans do not meet revenge with revenge. That Americans play by rules of human decency. That Americans are not those soldiers in the photos coming out of Abu Ghraib.

We start by demanding justice for the murder of Nick Berg, not vengeance for it. We start by drawing a line and saying the downward spiral of brutality ends here.

We start right in our own neighborhoods by trying to better understand people who are not like us.

There are demons in this world, and we saw some of them in the videotape of Nick Berg's murder. But mostly there are people—people not unlike you or me.

Understanding the difference between the two is the first step to winning the bigger war.

Trading Sides in Suburban Divide

It's spring in the suburbs, and that means it is home-improvement time.

Up and down neighborhood streets, decks are being built, additions going up, patios getting installed, and trees being planted.

In this nesting frenzy, two distinct and decidedly antagonistic nation-states have emerged: The State of Do-It-Yourselfers and the State of Hire-Its.

The Hire-Its live by the motto: "No job too small to pay a professional to do," the Do-It-Yourselfers by the words: "Just give me the right tool."

You can find the Do-It-Yourselfers out in force on any Saturday at Home Depot or Lowes, loading up on vast quantities of lumber, concrete, wiring, shrubs, fertilizer, flooring, and every other imaginable supply.

The Hire-Its can be found anywhere but Home Depot or Lowes. While the Do-It-Yourselfers are toiling away, the Hire-Its are usually out having fun, further fueling cross-tribal tensions.

The Do-It-Yourselfers sport tape measures as fashion accessories; the Hire-Its flash checkbooks with similar panache. The two sides, quite simply, detest each other.

The DIYs scoff dismissively at their unhandy neighbors who would not think twice about hiring an overpriced professional to, for instance, change a light bulb. DIYs collect power tools like trophies, and go through life enormously pleased with themselves.

The Great Divide

Across the back-fence divide, the HIs are just as smug. They believe there are two types of people in this world: those who do it right and those who try to do it themselves.

They harbor deep suspicions that the DIYs are bumbling amateurs whose substandard work is driving down property values. And they resent the fact that do-it-yourself projects stretch on interminably, lasting months, even years, and almost always involve unsightly mystery heaps piled in the driveway beneath blue tarps.

I have always considered myself a proud member in good standing of the do-it-yourself camp. Like my fellow DIYs, I am filled with unearned bravado, peppering conversations with such boasts as "Tear out a load-bearing wall to build a three-story atrium? Piece of cake!"

But recently I crossed enemy lines.

For five years my family has been lobbying to finish our basement so that it can be used for something other than storing potatoes. And for five years I have answered with that popular DIY battle cry: "It's on the list."

Then, a couple of months ago, my wife and three kids—closet Hire-Its all—ambushed me with a group intervention intended to make me admit I was in over my head, with a longer to-do list than even the most energetic DIY warrior could conquer.

My son reminded me that he had to wait two years for me to oil his squeaky door. My daughter piped up that her broken music box still sits on the workbench, in line behind the dismantled unicycle and toaster oven.

"Face it," my wife said. "By the time you get around to that basement, the kids will already have left home."

"So what's your point?" I asked.

A New Dawn

In the end I broke down and called a contractor. For the last few weeks, he and his helpers have been in and out of our house so much I'm beginning to think their real mission in life is to see how much dirt they can track in. We're all one big happy family.

But it's been hard on my ego.

The Do-It-Yourselfer in me wants to grab my tape measure and join them downstairs, bonding over miter cuts and drywall seams. The only job they need of me, however, is the one involving a pen and a blank check—and believe me, it's been keeping me busy.

I am a Hire-It turncoat, and, no, my DIY brethren, I'm not proud of it.

You can imagine my shame the other morning when the workers arrived at 7:00 A.M. sharp and caught me in the kitchen, still in my bathrobe. What kind of self-respecting do-it-yourself guy would not be dressed and on the job site by this leisurely hour?

They were all very polite, but I could see it on their faces: Yep, we're bailing out another hapless Hire-It.

My wife tries to talk me through my traitorous angst. The first time, she tells me, is always the hardest; the next hire will be much easier.

"Next?" I ask.

Sounds of Spring Roar in the 'Burbs

Outside my window, it looked like the Indianapolis 500—a sure sign that spring once again had returned to the suburbs.

From all directions came the roar of engines, the smell of exhaust, and the violent gnashing of blades.

Yes, folks, after a long peaceful winter, that darling of the suburban experience is back in force once again: grass-cutting season.

And last weekend, with its July-worthy temperatures, marked the unofficial but widely observed kickoff—the ceremonial first cut. Out where I live, this is no small deal.

I knew the big day had finally arrived when I awoke Saturday to the growl of Toros and John Deeres. Homeowners, start your engines!

Outside, up and down my street, I saw the same thing: Grown men (and a few women) perched on brightly colored riding mowers, zipping gleefully across the landscape at full throttle. Grass clippings flew, and the air held that sweet perfume of gasoline mixed with crushed chlorophyll.

Honestly, my neighbors looked ridiculous out there, perched on their low-riding mowing machines, knees up to their chests, like so many Shriners on go-carts.

My reaction was swift and predictable: "Dang! I've got to get out there!"

Conformity Calls

Here it was mid-April, and my tractor was still in the corner of the garage pinned beneath a pile of coiled hoses and folded lawn chairs. Late again. If I didn't want to get banned from the next neighborhood potluck, I knew I had better bring my shaggy lawn into compliance pronto.

So I spent my weekend—a gorgeous weekend, perfect for hiking or bicycling or simply snoozing in a hammock—on my knees in the garage, sharpening blades, tightening belts, and changing oil. And then with a roar and a cloud of blue smoke, I, too, was off to the races.

My lawn-less friends from the city just don't get it, this communal grass fanaticism. I'm hard-pressed to explain it myself, even as I spend two hours a week every week, April through October, embracing it.

It's totally crazy. And totally costly.

There is the price of the machines themselves, which can exceed that of a nice used automobile. There are the repairs and maintenance, the gasoline and fertilizer and pesticides. There are the hours—thousands of them each season in my subdivision alone—that could be spent doing better things. There are the costs to the environment, both from emissions and those millions of tiny gas spills.

And for what? A bumper crop that we neither eat nor sell nor even feed to our pets. With the fervor in which we grow this stuff, you would think we were all goat herders.

We fertilize it so it will grow like crazy, then we cut like crazy just to keep up. That leaves piles of clippings, which we rake and bag beneath the hot sun. And what do we do with this harvest? We place it on the curb and pay someone to haul it away.

Who's using whom?

It all makes you wonder who is actually calling the shots. Are we humans exploiting Kentucky bluegrass and fescue to tame our environment and improve our lives? Or are the grasses exploiting us to spread their dominion across the countryside? Think about it. When was the last time a blade of grass spent its hard-earned paycheck keeping you groomed?

A few hardy souls are fighting back. One couple I know replaced their sod with a native wildflower meadow that required no cutting, no fertilizers, no pesticides. You want to know how well the new look was embraced in their community? They were reported for creating a public nuisance.

I fight back in my own modest way, which is to say I follow the lazy man's guide to lawn care. It's strictly tough love: no fertilizers, no chemicals, no raking, no bagging. I cut it once a week, not a day more frequently.

Predictably, my lawn is a veritable United Nations of weeds. But they all get along reasonably well, and from a passing car at a certain speed, the overall effect keeps me just this side of banishment from the neighborhood association. The difference between the über suburban lawn and my own ragtag wannabe, I have found, comes down to this: twenty-five miles per hour.

A Soldier Returns, to Revelry, Relief

For fourteen months, Maria Murt did not dare allow herself to dream of the future. Her husband, Tom, a former Upper Moreland Township commissioner, had been plucked from her life to fight in Iraq.

Until she had him safely back home, the future would stay on hold.

She soldiered on, day by day, in her new role as single parent to three children, avoiding news programs and cringing each time the doorbell rang, afraid of the message that might arrive.

A week ago today, the Upper Moreland woman finally allowed herself to exhale. Standing in Philadelphia International Airport, she saw her soldier husband making his way toward her through the crowd.

"Tom!" she screamed. And they fell into each other's arms, neither able to say a word. Their three children—Katie, eleven, Daniel, nine, and Patrick, six—swarmed around. Murt's father, James, a World War II veteran, was there, too, and so was a color guard from the Willow Grove post of the Veterans of Foreign Wars.

"We were all just so emotional," Tom Murt, forty-four, said from home this week. "We were all crying."

The entire time Murt had been overseas, he was able to speak on the phone with the children just three times. On his first night home, Murt read bedtime stories to them, and the next morning he helped make their lunches and walked them to the bus stop. "That's what I missed the most," he said, "the simple, everyday parent things."

The hardest part of his deployment was not the scorpions or the pit toilets or the constant threat of attack. "The really, really hardest part is being away from your loved ones," he said.

As I reported February 23, Staff Sergeant Murt coped with the loneliness and boredom by launching a personal crusade to help the impoverished Iraqi children in the villages around his base. He sent e-mails home to friends and colleagues, asking them to donate whatever they could, and the local community responded in force. By the time he left, Murt had received and distributed more than two hundred large boxes of clothing, toys, and school supplies. In the process, he befriended hundreds of Iraqi children and built inestimable goodwill.

He could not wait to return to his own family, but part of his heart remains behind with the children he will never forget. "Once you see that kind of poverty," he said, "it's really very hard to stop thinking about it."

But now he is home, and home is where he plans to stay. He will not start back at his job as an instructor and academic adviser at Pennsylvania State University's Abington campus for several weeks. He said he had no plans to try to regain his seat on the Upper Moreland Board of Commissioners, which he resigned when he was deployed.

"We never expected it to be this long," Maria Murt said of their separation. "But we're together again. We're back as a unit. I just feel so lucky to have him home again."

She has seen the flag-draped coffins and knows how differently their story could have ended.

On his first morning home, right after putting the children on the bus to school, Tom and Maria Murt attended 9:00 A.M. Mass at St. David's Catholic Church in Willow Grove, where they are parishioners. They both had a few things for which to give thanks.

For Murt, the adjustment to civilian life will take time. His appetite is spotty, he continues to sleep fitfully, and loud noises bother him. His wife hopes her home cooking will help him regain some of the forty pounds he lost in the Iraq desert.

On a recent afternoon, Murt stepped out onto the front porch of the family home to greet yet another well-wisher. His children were clutched around him, not about to let him out of their sight again. It was an American portrait—a soldier home from war, a family made whole again.

Beside him, a large white banner flapped in the breeze. It read: "Welcome home, Tom. We love you and we are proud of you."

Ordinary People Vowing to Marry

In many ways, they are a typical suburban couple.

They spend their weekends remodeling their tidy three-bedroom house, which sits on a quiet street in the Main Line community of Strafford. They enjoy gardening and cooking and spoiling their dog, Cybil.

They both come from large, traditional Catholic families, and they dote on their seventeen nieces and nephews.

Now in their early fifties, they prefer quiet nights at home to going out on the town. They pay their taxes on time, look in on sick neighbors, and vote each election.

They are ordinary in all ways but one: Tim Dineen and Victor Martorano, a couple for nine years, are homosexuals. And that puts them squarely in the middle of the national debate on same-sex marriage.

They are not the ones protesting on courthouse steps or trying to force change by seeking marriage licenses where they know none will be issued. As the debate rages, they have written letters to newspapers, but otherwise go quietly about their suburban lives. It was for this reason—their very ordinariness—that I sought them out last week. I wanted to see for myself just how different from the heterosexual majority a gay couple in a long-term relationship is.

Marriage of the Minds

They give me a tour of their house and show off improvements they have made—new tile, enlarged kitchen, hardwood floors. On the table is a vase of pussy willows brought in from the garden. Outside, a pile of rain gutters sits in the yard, next weekend's project.

In their own minds, Dineen, a demonstration chef at a Trader Joe's market in nearby Wayne, and Martorano, who works in the travel industry, already are married. On their first Christmas together, they privately exchanged gold bands that have remained on their left ring fingers ever since. Still, says Dineen, "We will get married the day we legally can do it."

Some of the motivation is practical. If one is incapacitated, the other right now would need a written power of attorney to make medical decisions—a precaution they already have taken. And as Dineen pointed out over a cup of coffee, "If Victor died tomorrow, I would have to pay inheritance tax on his half of our house."

Adds Martorano: "The law does not recognize me as his next of kin, and that is wrong. It's just wrong."

But more important to the couple is what marriage stands for—a public acknowledgment of a couple's love and lifelong commitment. "Marriage is a stabilizing force in society," Dineen says, "and we want to be part of that stabilization."

After all, they consider themselves solid members of the community. And so do their neighbors. As Peg Schwartz, seventy-three and a registered Republican, told me later: "I can't say enough about them. They really could not be better neighbors. They are delightful. They're just nice, kind, caring people, and that's what you want in a neighbor." Having them next door has softened her position on gay marriage, she said. "If that makes them happy, then that's all that counts."

Battling Stereotypes

And yet, for now at least, Dineen and Martorano will remain the one couple on their street for whom the civil contract of marriage is not an option. Until that day comes, the two men believe stereotypes and prejudice will continue.

"Gay people have a reputation for being extremely promiscuous," says Dineen, whose full beard and wire-framed glasses give him a professorial air. "Well, not all gay people are."

Some of them lead their lives not much differently from the straight people on their streets, sharing the same worries and joys and dreams. And that brings Dineen to his main point.

"If we were married tomorrow, the only thing that would be different would be the piece of paper that grants us our rights and responsibilities. Nothing else would change. We would still be here just as we are today, putting new gutters on the house, going to work, grocery shopping, taking the dog to the vet."

He adds: "I think that's what so many people fail to realize. We're here already. We're a couple already. For all intents and purposes, we are married. We just lack the legalities."

An Escape on the Perkiomen Trail

Before the snows rolled in last week, I abandoned the express-way for one glorious day to experience a commute of an entirely different kind.

Perched on my rusty, trusty bicycle and carrying a bagged lunch, I set off beneath a brilliant late-winter sky to ride the new Perkiomen Trail.

The trail, completed in November at a cost of $9.7 million, cuts a nineteen-mile swath through Montgomery County, mostly hugging the lovely and largely unspoiled Perkiomen Creek.

My journey began in Green Lane Park, where the trail begins. Melting snow had left the path sodden, and I had gone only a few hundred yards before I was splattered from the chest

down in mud. B˙˙˙ ˙idn't care. The sun was out, the hint of
sprin˙˙ was playing hooky from work. Bring

U·S AIRWAYS

Name of Passenger
GLASSMOYER/AMY ZONE 3
CWY2JP/US
CONF:
FFD:
SAN DIEGO Date
PHOENIX
Flight DEPARTS 27APR
231 645A Seat
Boarding Time 5F
Gate
37 615A

˙kiomen Creek swirled around boul-
˙aters catching the glint of sunlight
˙e branches. Ahead, the trail, on a
˙d off into the woods, and I could
˙e path less traveled.
˙n horseback and a few solitary
˙trail all to myself.

˙e Paradise

˙me homeowners along the
˙ic trail. Theirs was a small
p˙ ˙s and stone farmhouses sat
pe˙ ˙ove the creek—and now their owners
fac˙ ˙ue of strangers trudging past, peering into their
lives.

I did not blame them for being upset—but they are wrong.
The public good in this instance far outweighs the loss of privacy enjoyed by a few.

The trail was well-marked, but in the tiny berg of Spring
Mount I somehow made a wrong turn and ended up taking a
five-mile detour on hilly, paved roads, including a white-
knuckle jaunt down busy Route 29, before rejoining the trail
in Schwenksville.

But even getting lost can have its serendipitous joys. Just
outside the village of Zieglerville, I came across a tiny, seemingly forgotten walled cemetery, its time-worn gravestones
chiseled in German, a reminder of this region's immigrant
roots.

If some residents hated the idea of the trail, the businesses along this hardscrabble strip love it. The trail offers them their best hope at rejuvenation, and many have turned their gazes out their back doors, toward the river and trail, putting out picnic tables and welcome signs to encourage trail users to stop—and spend.

I did neither, pushing on toward my ultimate destination—the trail's terminus in Valley Forge National Historical Park where it merges into the Schuylkill River Trail.

Not Quite Pristine

Near Graterford Prison, where signs warn you to stay on the trail, I wound my way through a gentle wetlands and beneath a magnificent sycamore tree, its pale, peeling bark aglow in the sunlight.

No one would call this trail pristine, although stretches of it certainly come close. My trip took me past mossy boulders and junked cars, past serene stands of oaks and trash-strewn factories. Past honking geese and buzzing electrical substations.

And no one would call it a wilderness experience, either. I stopped and did my banking along the way, and could have gotten a Big Mac or Chinese take-out, too, had I wanted.

But the overall effect was one seldom found in the teeming suburbs, and that was a sense of being loose in a special place where the pulse of nature, despite the concrete and steel all around it, still beats a lively patter.

This trail travels not only through space, from north to south, but through time, as well, harkening to the generations that came before.

As I wandered into Lower Perkiomen Valley Park, near the conclusion of my journey, it occurred to me that the shortest path between two points is not always the best. In our rush-through-the-day world, the slow, meandering trail can be a salve for the soul.

At the trail's end, I hopped off my bike and dug out my cell phone. Tired, sweaty, and utterly content, I dialed the emergency response team that I knew was on standby. "Honey," I asked, "could you come pick me up?"

An Oasis of Sanity on Gay Marriage

I came to the historic riverfront town of New Hope expecting to find Gomorrah on the Delaware, its populace turned to pillars of salt for daring to so brazenly embrace homosexual union.

But on Friday, three days after the Borough Council unanimously voted in favor of gay marriage, all was quiet.

Tourists—the few who were out on this blustery day—strolled the cobblestone lanes. Shoppers browsed. Carpenters hammered. Bakers baked. Waiters waited on lunch customers.

Not a salt pillar in sight.

Up and down the streets, residents and workers reacted the same way to last Tuesday's resolution, which read in part: "Now, be it hereby resolved that the New Hope Borough Council supports the issuance of marriage licenses to gay and lesbian couples and calls upon the County of Bucks and the Commonwealth of Pennsylvania to issue such licenses."

They said it was no big deal.

"To each their own," said P. J. Fischer, twenty-seven, a heterosexual who manages the clothing store Savioni. "Shouldn't they have a right to be happy?"

"I don't mind at all," said Kate Hudson, twenty-six, of East Norriton, as she walked out of Starbucks. "I don't feel anyone has a right to tell anyone else how to live their lives."

At Gerenser's Exotic Ice Cream, manager Beau Johnson, thirty-two, shrugged off the controversy. "I'm straight, but I have no problem with it," he said.

A tourist from Virginia added: "There shouldn't be a law against love."

Equal, but Not Quite

The council's vote came after a gay resident, Stephen Stahl, fifty-four, stood up at Tuesday's council meeting and asked, as he put it, "a simple question: How do you apply for a marriage license?"

The answer, for those who seek to tie the knot with someone of the same sex, is, "You don't."

Despite that, Stahl and his partner of twenty-eight years, Robert Seneca, forty-eight, plan to force the issue today when they will attempt to seek a marriage license at the Bucks County Courthouse.

They know they will be turned away, they told me as we sat in Stahl's cozy writing studio on Main Street.

"It's really not about Robert and me," said Stahl, a playwright. "It's about [gay] people who will follow. In twenty-five years, we'll all be laughing about this. Things will change."

His partner added: "Just not soon enough."

Marriage, they said, carries certain guaranteed privileges, for instance involving taxes and inheritance and rights of survivorship. Their fight is about equal rights, but something more.

"It's about that word, marriage," Stahl said. "I'm looking for the word."

Stahl is a local Republican committeeman, but he said he would resign the post today in protest of what he sees as his party's radical reactionary swing under President Bush.

A Small First Step

Before heading out of town, I talked with two council members, Sharyn Keiser, a lesbian who has been in the same relationship for seventeen years, and Ed Duffy, who is married. They agreed that little New Hope's journey into this divisive national issue is quixotic, yet worth taking.

"Are we going to turn things around immediately?" Keiser asked. "No. But we're making a statement that will be heard."

As an elected official, Duffy said, he can no longer sit back without insisting that gay couples "be able to enjoy the same rights as everyone else."

As I drove out of town, I found myself agreeing with him. This country was built on a healthy separation of church and state. No religion is forced to recognize, let alone bless, any marital union. The government, on the other hand, has an obligation to offer its legal institutions, including marriage, to all Americans, not just those who fit accepted social mores.

Substitute any other population group for denial—no white-black marriages, no Jewish-Gentile marriages, no native-immigrant marriages—and you have what this is really all about, which is prejudice.

Besides, given the divorce rate and the reckless whimsy with which so many straight couples march down the wedding aisle, homosexuals cannot possibly make a bigger mockery of the institution than we heterosexuals already have.

You Just Can't Shut Down
That Surf-Music Sound

If you have never heard of the Rip Chords, you are forgiven. Neither had I.

But if you were a teenager cruising America's highways with your radio on in 1964, you undoubtedly heard their one big hit, "Hey, Little Cobra."

It was a hot-rod anthem in the tradition of "Little Deuce Coupe" and "409," with Beach Boys–style harmonies over a driving surf-guitar riff. And in that time, before the country was torn open by Vietnam and social turmoil, it was near the top of the charts.

Bands like the Rip Chords are known as "one-hit wonders." They rise, flame out, and are never heard of again.

But forty years later, the Rip Chords are back—and in a place no less improbable than a strip shopping center in Northeast Philadelphia.

Drive down Bustleton Avenue on a Wednesday night and walk into Dr. Robert Rush's chiropractic office. Take the steps to the basement and there, in a back room crowded with drums and amplifiers, you'll find the band's current lineup, tuning up, ready to let loose one more time.

They're not kids anymore, of course. Their hair has grayed and receded. Waistlines have thickened. Reading glasses hang from necks. They have day jobs. Their only groupies these days, they joke, are their wives and children.

But what's important, they tell you, is that they are playing again—and people are turning out to listen.

The story of the Rip Chords' long and painful climb out of obscurity is a story of shattered dreams, crushing disappointment, and, ultimately, of friendship and redemption.

And it begins with the rotund, balding man standing in the middle of the rehearsal room, tambourine in hand. His name is Richie Rotkin, and in 1963 he was one of the original front men in the Rip Chords, a band that was the creation of two Los Angeles music producers who wanted to capitalize on the surf-music sound.

For two heady summers, Rotkin rode the crest of fame. He appeared on *American Bandstand* and remembers traveling on tour in a Dick Clark–sponsored revue with the Supremes and other stars.

But by late 1964, the run was over. And Rotkin, with no rights to royalties and no prospects for a new gig, was washed up. The Southern Californian married his sweetheart and moved with her back to her hometown of Philadelphia, where he found employment in a decidedly less glamorous segment of the entertainment industry—working for a vending company that supplies pinball machines and pool tables. He still works there today.

"It was just crushing," said Rotkin, now a sixty-two-year-old grandfather in Southampton in Lower Bucks County. "I walked away from it."

For more than thirty years he tried to shut the door on his brief flirtation with fame. He stopped singing and couldn't attend a concert without tears welling in his eyes, remembering what it felt like to be the one on stage.

Then, seven years ago, a mutual friend introduced Rotkin to Rush, the chiropractor, and they became fast friends.

Rush, of New Hope, grew up in the Northeast and for years had played in area rock bands. So, too, had two of his best childhood friends, Fred Brog, a psychologist who works in Chester County, and Mitchell Schecter, of the Northeast, who teaches music.

The three friends, all fifty-one, knew all about the Rip Chords. They talked Rotkin into joining them for an informal jam session, and the reconstituted Rip Chords was born.

The trademark on the band's name had long ago expired, and they snatched it up. They bought matching Hawaiian shirts to perform in.

Soon they discovered the market for nostalgia bands, and began getting paying gigs around the country at auto shows, casinos, festivals, and state fairs, sometimes sharing billing with other all-but-forgotten oldies bands such as the Archies, the Orlons and the Surfaris.

They recruited a second original Rip Chords member, Arnie Marcus, sixty-one, now an actor in Los Angeles, to join them for major appearances. Recently, they added a talented drummer, Patrick Maley, twenty-nine, whose parents used to listen to the Rip Chords.

The band's crowning glory came last year when it was invited to play at a nostalgia-rock revue in Austin, Texas, which was broadcast nationally on PBS in November. The crowd gave them a standing ovation.

Rotkin concedes he's an emotional man, and when he later watched the concert on television, he began to weep. After a lonely, four-decade exile, he was back.

"Richie is one of the sweetest people in the whole world, and he got really beat up [by the music industry] back in the sixties," said Rush, who acts as the band's manager. "My goal for him, I said, [was] 'Richie, I'm going to help you get your life back for you.' It makes me real proud to know I kind of took the thorn out of the lion's paw."

When they get together to rehearse, they spend a lot of time gushing about the great blasts from the past they once idolized and now rub shoulders with—Jan & Dean, Fabian, the Spencer Davis Group, Peter Noone of Herman's Hermits, Al Jardine of the Beach Boys.

It might all be just a little sad if they weren't having so much fun. "We feel like we're fourteen again," Rush said.

I tell them I'm not leaving until they perform the hit that began it all, and they gladly oblige.

When the first chord of "Hey, Little Cobra" rings out, their faces light up like neon. They grin, they beam, they bounce. Joy like this cannot be faked. These are five happy guys, rockin' their way into the sunset, creaky knees and all.

A Boy's Fantasy Vs. a Postal Robot

At the Marano home in South Philadelphia, the holiday decorations are stashed away for another season, but Santa still dominates conversation.

Specifically, the family is trying to understand how a five-year-old's letter addressed to "Santa Claus, North Pole" could be returned for insufficient postage. And, they ask, just what exactly is sufficient postage to an imaginary place on top of the world?

Our tale of Yuletide disappointment begins in mid-December when Zachary Marano, a kindergartner at Our Lady of Angels

Catholic School, decided to draw Santa a map to his home on South 30th Street.

With the help of his grandmother, Patricia Marano, who watches him each afternoon while his parents, Christopher and Michelle Marano, are at work, he addressed the envelope to the North Pole and stuck on stickers—but no stamp. She then drove him to the nearby Point Breeze Post Office on Snyder Avenue where he dropped it into the mail slot.

Mission accomplished, or so the boy thought.

On Christmas Eve, Zachary scattered "magic oats" on the lawn for Santa's reindeer, and after he was asleep, his father sneaked out to make hoof prints in the dirt.

Santa indeed filled the Marano home with toys, and Zachary chalked it up to his ace map-drawing skills.

Until last week, that is, when he returned home from school, fetched the mail, and found his unopened letter to Santa, stamped "Return to Sender."

Making Excuses

A disappointed Zachary looked up at his grandmother and asked, "Didn't Santa Claus get my letter?"

"I said, 'I'm sure he got your letter. Maybe he read it and sent it back to you,'" Patricia Marano recalled.

But the grandmother was steamed. What could postal workers have been thinking, returning a child's letter to Santa? How could they not notice it was addressed to a polar ice cap?

She called the Point Breeze station, where she says a clerk told her flatly that all unstamped mail is returned.

"I said, 'We're talking Santa Claus here,'" she recounted.

Zachary's father was upset, too.

"It was just the most bizarre thing," he said. "We figured it would go where all the other letters to Santa Claus go, or that they would just throw it away. The whole point was for Zachary to believe that Santa was going to get it and fulfill his wishes."

Marano talked to a supervisor who told him he did not know how the letter ended up being returned.

"They weren't very apologetic," Marano said. "They basically said these things happen."

Manager Joe Kelly told me the same thing this week. "I don't know how that happened. I've been here doing this thirty-five years, and this is the first time I've ever heard of [a Santa letter being returned]," Kelly said. "We just send them to the Santa Claus office at 30th and Market."

Blame It on Automation

I must admit, as I listened to the Maranos describe the letter snafu, I imagined an inept government clerk mindlessly stamping "Return to Sender" on any letter without a stamp.

But Donna DiLacqua, the Postal Service's spokeswoman for Greater Philadelphia, assured me the culprit almost certainly was not a bonehead human but a sorting machine, which automatically spat out the no-stamp envelope and routed it back to its sender.

Zachary's envelope had the return address on the back, and the machine, as designed, flipped the envelope so the back side faced up, DiLacqua said. The mail carrier, knowing it was a "return to sender" piece, would not bother looking at the original address.

"It was just an honest mistake," she said. Of the thousands of Santa letters the Philadelphia area postal system received this

holiday, Zachary's is the only one she knows of that was returned by mistake.

And thus concludes this postholiday tempest. Zachary's faith
in Santa remains unshaken. His parents and grandmother,
while still miffed, realize bureaucratic bungles can get a lot
worse than this one. And the Postal Service is reminded that
what it does matters—especially when it does it wrong.

Next year, the Maranos say, they'll do one thing differently
for sure.

No return address.

They're Bad, and We Love 'em Still

Man, and I thought my dog was bad.

Ever since I penned a farewell to my companion of thirteen
years, Marley the neurotic and incorrigible Labrador retriever,
my e-mail inbox has resembled a TV talk show episode: "Bad
Dogs—and the Humans Who Love Them!"

In the week since I wrote about Marley's death, I have
heard from several hundred pet owners. They offered condo-
lences (thanks, everyone). But mostly they wanted to dispute
the accuracy of my report.

Now I know I erred when I characterized Marley as the
planet's worst-behaved creature. The typical response went
something like, "Your dog could not have been the worst because MY dog is the worst." And to prove the point, they sup-
plied detailed accounts of shredded couches, raided cupboards,
and sneak slobber attacks.

Oddly enough, nearly all the tales involved large retrievers, just like Marley.

Take it away, Sandy Chanoff of Abington Township: "Alex was what we called a 'high-spirited Lab' with a little attention deficit disorder. He ate almost all of my leather shoes, pocketbooks, and even the carpet. He would greet us at the door with something in his mouth all the time, and would jump all around like he hadn't seen us in years. He knocked everything off the coffee table with his tail. By the way, we were also thrown out of obedience school." You, too, huh?

Diploma Envy

Gracie, a golden retriever owned by Lynne Major and Lynn Lampman of Drexel Hill, actually managed to graduate—and was so excited she promptly jumped up and pulverized her diploma. Said Major: "She is lovable and a little crazy at the same time."

Lois Finegan of Upper Darby said my manic mutt had nothing on her separation-anxiety-challenged Lab, Gypsy. "She was a holy terror in her day, eating curtains and their rods, doors, rugs, plants, and even a jalousie window."

Others reported their dogs gobbling down beach towels, sponges, kitty litter, spare change, even a diamond ring (which definitely trumps Marley's taste for gold necklaces).

Mike Casey of Pottstown beat them all. He said his late dog, Jason, a retriever-Irish setter mix, once downed a five-foot vacuum cleaner hose, coiled reinforcing wire and all—without so much as a burp.

Elyssa Burke of West Goshen feared the worst after her dog, Mo (yes, another highly intelligent Lab!), decided to exit the house by crashing through a second-story window. Mo survived the fall just fine, apparently quite delighted by his newly forged egress. "He landed on a shrub, which broke his fall," Burke explained.

Nancy Williams clipped my column on Marley because it reminded her of her own irrepressible retriever, Gracie. She writes: "I left the article on the kitchen table and turned to put away the scissors. When I turned back, sure enough, Gracie had eaten the column."

I'll take that as a compliment.

Knee-Deep in Concrete

Rene Wick of Havertown owns "a lunk-headed yellow Lab named Clancy," who decided to make a lasting impression on the next-door neighbors by visiting their newly poured foundation. "Clancy jumped the fence and went straight into the still-wet concrete up to his knees," Wick wrote.

And then came Haydon, the brawny—not to be confused with brainy—Lab that once swallowed a tube of Super Glue. "His finest hour, however," owner Carolyn Etherington of Jamison recounted, "was when he tore the frame out of the garage door after I had foolishly attached his leash to it." She adds, "In those days, we had the veterinarian on speed dial."

Tim Manning of Yardley thought he had outfoxed his yellow Lab, Ralph, by stowing a chocolate centerpiece safely on top of the refrigerator. "Ralph figured out how to open a drawer on the linen cabinet next to the refrigerator and use it as a ladder," Manning wrote. "We could tell because the drawer's contents were all over the floor, and the chocolate was devoured right there on top of the fridge."

All of which raises the question that any sane person must be asking: If pets are this much of a pain, why does anyone keep them?

As Sharon Durivage of Yardley put it: "They give their love and loyalty freely and always forgive us for our bad days and cranky moods."

The Columnist's Life Is Not Easy

Recently I received a lengthy survey from an Australian psychologist studying how journalists are affected by trauma on the job.

The more than two hundred questions aim to document and better understand post-traumatic stress disorder symptoms in newspaper and television reporters and photographers who wade daily into the harsh realities of a brutal world.

As a columnist on the suburban beat, let me tell you, I have plenty to report. It's a jungle out there.

I'm still waking in cold sweats from my close encounter with the Lilly Pulitzer spring-fashion sale at the Valley Forge Convention Center. All those too-tanned women, all that too-perky pastel. It's just too vivid.

Then there was the opening of the new Ikea store near Conshohocken. You haven't tasted fear until you've found yourself standing between two hundred crazed suburban shoppers and the cookware sales rack on opening day. The distant, glazed look in their eyes haunts me to this day.

I don't even want to recount my foray into Bed, Bath &
Beyond. Suffice it to say I will never again be able to face the
words *white sale.*

A Time to Reflect

Coincidentally, the trauma survey arrived on my desk just as I
was celebrating my one-year anniversary here at the *Inquirer.*
As I worked through the questions, the flashbacks from deep
inside suburbia rained down like mortars. The angry soccer
moms. The hyper Little League dads. The sneers of bored
teenagers. The eerie glow of tanning salons. And always, re-
lentlessly, the dull resounding thud of randomly whacked golf
balls: "Incoming!"

Oh, the tragic face-lifts I have seen! Oh, the bad dye jobs!

You might think the suburban beat a tame beast. True, I
never have witnessed real combat, but I was at the front lines
when the Washington Crossing re-enactors nearly unleashed
musket volleys over who would ride in which boats across the
Delaware. Images that ugly do not soon fade.

I have squinted into the E-Z Pass lanes' blinding blue blaze
and braved suburbia's twisted roads to nowhere. I have dodged
delirious SUV drivers and flying trash cans launched from the
beds of landscape trucks. Unflinchingly, I have confronted
those four most dreaded words of the suburban experience:
Roadwork ahead; merge left.

One day I stared into the face of death—and staring back
was a Hummer with a sixteen-year-old at the wheel.

Like, dude, pick a lane.

My suburban stress began with a twitch and blossomed into
uncontrollable spasms. Never a good thing when you're merging
onto the Blue Route with a twenty-ounce Wawa coffee in hand.

Answering the researchers' questions brought to the surface months of suppressed anxiety.

Unspeakable Horrors

"Did you ever witness a particularly gruesome scene while covering an assignment?" the survey asks. I can't speak about it except to say it involved two moms, two minivans, and one parking space in front of Target.

"Have you been in a war zone?" it asked. Does the King of Prussia mall the week before Christmas count?

"Have you been attacked with a weapon other than in combat?" You must be referring to the grandmother with the shopping cart in the Genuardi's produce aisle.

"Were you ever physically attacked while on assignment?" That would be the day I accompanied Miss Poop, the Main Line's pooper-scooper entrepreneur, as she made her rounds through the backyards of mansions. Why oh why did the lady in the bathrobe let her four Dobermans out like that?

"Some people have the experience of feeling that other people and the world around them are not real. Has this happened to you?" Only when I'm at a Darby Borough meeting.

"Were you ever verbally threatened while covering an assignment?" Well, of course I was, but not to worry. That's just our regional way of saying, "Howdy, neighbor!"

The survey asks a lot about recurring dreams, and, yes, I'm haunted by one of those, too: I've driven into a planned suburban development—AND I CAN'T GET OUT!

No matter which direction I turn, I always end up back in the same place.

Trapped for life on Periwinkle Lane.

Bad Behavior Has No Zip Code

Some weeks the suburbs seem like an oasis of serenity in a troubled world.

Other weeks, they more resemble a jungle of tangled dysfunction. The last couple have been real doozies. The headlines read like the pilot for a new Fox reality show, *Suburban Meltdown*. Coming soon to a family therapy session near you.

Foster parents duct-taping babies. Soccer dads punching out coaches. Child-corrupting party moms heading off to prison. Teachers seducing students. Coaches seducing players. Mothers driving getaway cars for their sons' crimes. Oh, and did we mention the Pine Sol in the sippy cup?

It's enough to make you scratch your head and ask, "If this is what people are fleeing to, what are they fleeing from?"

Where to Begin?

In King of Prussia, a woman is arrested on a shoplifting charge and taken to jail. What she doesn't tell police is that she left her year-old son locked alone inside her apartment in Norristown. Two days later, police find the baby, dehydrated and with diaper rash but otherwise unhurt.

Hello? Earth to mom? Come in, mom? Please report to lost-and-found to retrieve your maternal instinct.

Soccer Dads on the Edge

In Northampton Township, Bucks County, Villa Joseph Marie girls' soccer coach John McOwen receives a concussion when he allegedly is decked by the father of a player in a dispute over how much field time the girl is getting. Well, that's one way to teach the kids conflict resolution.

Meanwhile, a Montgomery County woman admits to driving the getaway truck for her son and another teenager in the heist of $56,000 worth of laptop computers from a Hatfield elementary school. The best part: Police say mother and son hid the loot in the pool house at her East Norriton residence. Pool house? She can afford a place with a pool house, and she's out helping junior steal from school kids?

Of course, she had a good reason. Bonnie Lohin, according to authorities, was helping her son raise money so he could repay her for a car. Gee, whatever happened to getting a job?

Adding to the plot line of our suburban soap opera, a former Phoenixville High School English teacher was sent to prison last week for having a sexual relationship with a student. And a former lacrosse coach awaited a possible prison sentence of her own on her guilty plea to having sex with two underage boys and hosting drinking parties for teens she met while coaching her thirteen-year-old son's team.

If that's not tawdry enough, the queen of suburban meltdowns herself, Megan Smith, was sent to prison Thursday for staging a teen drinking party in her Willow Grove home, in which a girl says she was sexually assaulted, and for renting a motel room for her then-fourteen-year-old daughter and the girl's boyfriend.

Excuse me, but are there any grownups left around here?

Babies Bound in Tape

Then there was the pitiful case of the foster children bound like mummies in duct tape in a Levittown home. A Bucks

County jury last week found Colleen Broe not guilty of illegally wrapping the two toddlers, one and two, in tape as a way to restrain them.

But the acquittal more reflected doubt over what role Broe's estranged husband, who admitted photographing the bound babies, played in the taping than an endorsement of her parenting. Broe admitted lying to social workers about her unstable marriage. Her own children testified they saw her taping the babies, but she said she used the duct tape only to keep the toddlers from opening their diapers. (Hasn't she ever heard of one-piece outfits that zip from behind?)

In defending herself, Broe described a home life in an utter tailspin.

Once, she testified, she found the babies' cups spiked with Pine Sol and suspected her husband of trying to poison them. Yet she did not call police or social workers.

Just another blissful day in paradise.

There are many good reasons to move to the suburbs, but, as these last couple weeks have shown, escaping bad behavior is not one of them.

If that's why you're fleeing the city, you'd best keep driving. And don't stop until you hit the Arctic Circle.

Dining in Style, Thanks to You All

"Table for two, please," I said.

The tuxedoed maitre d' led us past the wood-fired grill, the slabs of aged beef, and the iced tubs of imported Mediterranean fish to a linen-draped seating overlooking the Delaware River.

We opened our menus.

"Wow!" my wife said.

"Pay no attention to the prices," I told her. "This meal is on the taxpayers of Pennsylvania."

Or at least we could pretend. We were at La Veranda Ristorante, the unapologetically high-end eatery near Penn's Landing. It's where State Senator Vincent J. Fumo (D-Philadelphia) managed to rack up $72,525 in dinner bills over a two-year period—101 visits in all, sometimes with dozens of guests. Fumo charged it all to the people of Pennsylvania through a discretionary fund available to top legislative leaders.

Does this guy have an appetite or what?

The South Philly Democratic heavyweight does not want to talk about his publicly financed meal deals. Nor will he identify the guests he brought to La Veranda, sometimes thirty or more at a time. But he did say through a spokesman that he uses the meals to discuss the public's business.

And as I sat in La Veranda, sailboats bobbing at their moorings outside my window, Sinatra crooning in the background, I could just hear the discourse: "Hmmmm, how should we sock it to the public tonight? The lobster tail with baby Mediterranean shrimp in cognac at $43.95 or the surf and turf at $45?"

If Not Me, Then Who?

In a state where the words financial and crisis always seem to go hand in hand, how could one public servant possibly expend such a fortune on fine dining? My assignment—a tough one, but someone had to step forward—was to eat my way to the truth. Waistline be damned, I was going to chow down like a Pennsylvania politician.

Franco, our waiter, started us off with fresh bruschetta and grilled vegetables; he handed me an eighteen-page wine list.

The first bottle I spotted carried a price tag of $350. Whoa! Taxpayers of Chester County, here's mud in your eye!

But wait. Being a responsible steward of the public trust—and because alcohol is the one thing Fumo and other legislative leaders are not allowed to ring up on the taxpayers' dime—I opted instead to slum with the second-cheapest bottle on the list, an Italian Merlot for $34. Hey, Vince, how am I doing so far?

Franco suggested we whet our appetites with the grilled langostino, or prawns, grilled over open flames and drizzled with olive oil. Normally, as a civilian cheapskate, I would choke on those two dreaded words, market price. But this was Fumo Fantasyland, and we all know a hungry legislator is a grumpy legislator. C'mon, taxpayers, what do you say? I squeezed my wife's hand to calm her private-sector jitters. "Bring 'em on, Franco," I said.

At $34, I later learned, the langostino worked out to about $3 per bite—but what bites they were. ("A great big *'Grazie'* to the generous taxpayers of Erie.")

A Memorable Evening

For our entrées, Franco recommended choice selections of imported fish, baked in a heavy salt crust. Again, we faced the mystery market price, but I had stopped sweating the details after the second glass of wine. The fish was divine, and so were the rosemary roasted potatoes and wilted greens.

We ate. We drank. We lingered. We discussed the public's business. ("I wonder what the little people of Scranton are having for dinner tonight.") We let out our belts.

Of course, there was room for dessert ("Thank you, Pittsburgh!"), cappuccinos ("You really shouldn't have, Norristown!"), and a wonderful lemon liquor Franco brought out on the house because we were turning out to be such good, Fumo-worthy customers.

It was a meal to remember. And at just under $200 with the wine and tip on my *Inquirer* expense account, I'm sure my boss won't let me forget it for years to come. (Note to Finance Department: We had no fun whatsoever.)

On the way out, Franco shook my hand and said, "Please come see us again."

"We sure will," I said. Of course, first I need to get elected.

Lessons to Avoid a Homeless Future

The woman stood before King of Prussia District Justice William Maruszczak and pleaded poverty.

She was sixty-two years old, had worked her entire life. And here she was, just a few months after losing her secretarial job, unable to pay her rent.

The landlord wanted her out.

The judge granted the eviction, wondering: "How can you be sixty-two years old and still not have anything?"

He assumed she would be taken in by relatives. But weeks later, he learned she was homeless. "Somebody who worked for forty years is living in a car? How does this happen?"

It's a question Maruszczak has asked countless times during his six years as a district justice. The cases come before him on an almost daily basis—people from all walks of life in financial meltdown. Many earn middle-income wages or better but managed to save nothing over years of working full-time.

"They're coming in front of me and they're broke," the judge said. And he wonders, "Well, what have you been doing for the last twenty years?"

The answer, he said, whether they earn $20,000 a year or $120,000, is spending more than they earn, often with the help of credit cards.

From his bench, he sees the personal face of a grim national statistic: more than 1.5 million Americans declared personal bankruptcy in the twelve months ending March 31—an all-time high. Millions more are living one step ahead of insolvency.

A Fragile Facade

We all know someone like this living the American dream atop a mountain of car leases, loans, and maxed-out credit cards. On the surface all is fine, but one missed paycheck and the cheery facade collapses.

Something needs to be done about this crisis of personal insolvency, the judge believes, and he and his friend John Garrett, a retired bond broker from Paoli, think they know what is needed: Required personal-finance training for every high school student in Pennsylvania.

"People aren't being taught at the most basic level that you need to live within your means and you need to put something away," Maruszczak said.

The idea is not new. It has gotten some attention in Congress, and the Philadelphia School District plans to build personal-finance lessons into middle and high school curricula next year. But currently just three states—Florida, Illinois and Rhode Island—require all students to complete mandatory money courses.

In Pennsylvania, many high schools offer money management as an elective, not a requirement. "This is as vital to your
life as your health is," Garrett said. Yet when he sent a letter to
eleven suburban school districts offering to put together a fi-
nance curriculum for them, he said he got nowhere.

So the men talk up the idea with whomever will listen, as I
did over lunch Monday. The idea makes sense. We teach children about literature and biology but not how to take the most
basic steps to remain solvent in life.

The Allure of Plastic

Credit-card companies make it easy for young adults to carry
plastic, and the average college student carries a monthly
credit-card tab of about $2,000, studies show. Couple that
with student and car loans, and many are deeply in debt before
they even enter the workplace.

Doesn't it make sense to teach young people how to manage debt before they find themselves buried by it?

Garrett and Maruszczak want to drive home the most fun-
damental of lessons: Spend less than you make; pay off your
credit cards each month; don't buy what you can't afford; sock
away a little of each paycheck; start saving young so your in-
vestments have time to appreciate.

Basic stuff, they admit, but apparently lost on many wage
earners.

As for the evicted woman living in her car, Maruszczak said
he helped her find a $400-a-month apartment, which she
could afford on her $900-a-month Social Security check.

He wonders how different her retirement might be today
had she invested a little of each paycheck over the years. After
all, even at secretary wages, he estimates she earned $2 million

during her career. A few basic lessons early in life could have paid huge dividends in the end.

～～～つ

A Message from One Foster Child

As special agent in charge of the FBI's Mobile, Alabama, field office, Timothy Munson does not have a lot of time to correspond with newspaper columnists.

Yet when he read my column about a young woman who went directly from the state's foster-care system to its welfare rolls as an unwed mother, the Philadelphia native felt compelled to share his own story.

Like the young woman I wrote about October 7, Munson grew up in the state's foster-care system and was passed from one home to the next. Like her, he was, by his teenage years, adrift and directionless.

Unlike her, he stumbled upon someone who believed in him, and with a lot of hard work, he managed to rise above his circumstances.

"Like it or not," said the West Philly foster-kid-turned-federal-agent, "I've become a role model"—especially for young African Americans.

Munson, fifty-five, was back in his hometown last week for a national law-enforcement conference, where he shared his story with me.

From his earliest memories, Tim Munson knew only foster care. He and a brother lived in a home on the 800 block of

Lex Street run by a strict woman who did not believe in sparing the rod. By today's standards, he said, she would be arrested for child abuse.

He knew nothing about his family.

A Soldier Appears

Then one day at Martha Washington Elementary School, a handsome soldier in full dress greens showed up and introduced himself as Munson's older brother. That's when the boy learned he was one of eleven children his mother had had by five fathers.

That brief meeting was a watershed for the boy. He had a family and a big brother who made him proud.

For the next several years, though, he continued to bump through life, living with a variety of relatives he barely knew, including, briefly, his mother.

It was then that fate touched him.

Munson earned money delivering the *Evening Bulletin*. One of his customers was Eugene Wayman Jones, a well-known African American intellectual in the city. Jones, a professor at Temple University, began to mentor the boy. And after Munson ran away from a particularly horrendous living arrangement, Jones took him in.

The educator offered the boy stability and introduced him to classical music, art, and literature. "He struck a spark in my life," Munson said.

It might have been a fairy-tale ending, except that Munson arrived home from Germantown High School one day to find his mentor dead of natural causes. Crushed, he again was bounced from one home to the next.

Off to Vietnam

"To be honest," he said, "I was falling apart." In 1965, at age seventeen, he dropped out of Germantown High, joined the army, and was sent to Vietnam. After his honorable discharge three years later, he still had no idea what to do with his life.

He earned his general equivalency diploma, began working in a restaurant, and fell in love with a shy girl named Alice. They married and settled in Mount Airy. In 1973, looking for more job security, he became a Philadelphia police officer. At the police academy, a lieutenant urged him to pursue a college degree on the GI Bill.

Munson had never considered college. But he was accepted at La Salle University, where six years later, working full time, he obtained a criminal justice degree.

In 1981, he took the test to join the FBI and, to his surprise, passed. He steadily moved up through the agency's ranks, and today supervises an office of more than a hundred agents and civilian employees in Mobile.

A strong proponent of two-parent families, he and his wife have been married for thirty-five years, and raised two sons who both earned college degrees and are in professional careers.

When he read my description of that young lost woman, he said, he recognized the path he might have taken if not for a few good souls who helped him believe in himself.

He often shares his story with schoolchildren in the hope they will learn from his experience. He also wants to encourage minorities to consider careers with the FBI.

His message is simple: "If I could make it, you can make it, too."

Her Frank Talk Could Save Lives

Maryann McCullough wants all of us to start talking about our bathroom habits.

She wants us to get comfortable using the words colon, rectum, and bowel movement, and to get over our bashfulness regarding this most private of human functions.

No, the Montgomery County mother of three does not have some scatological fetish. She's just trying to save a few lives.

She and her family learned the hard way that the deadliest aspect of one type of cancer in particular is the silence of shame that surrounds it. Colorectal cancer is the second-leading cancer killer in the United States after lung cancer. "But why don't you ever hear about it?" McCullough, forty, asked. "Because people don't want to talk about it. They're embarrassed by it. I don't know why breasts are OK to talk about but not rectums."

Her husband, Bob, a general contractor who grew up in Glenside and built the family's home in Maple Glen with his own hands, was one of those gregarious guys who, as his wife said, "could talk to anybody about anything."

But there was one topic he never spoke about—the growing discomfort deep in his bowels that had been bothering him for months.

Like many men, he didn't want to think about his personal plumbing, let alone talk about it—not to his family, not to his buddies, not to his doctors. The only sign of his distress was his habit of constantly sucking on antacids.

An Upset Stomach

When his wife would ask if he was feeling OK, he would euphemistically reply that he had a little upset stomach. The truth was the pain was below his stomach, in his digestive tract, where he experienced bloating, gas, and difficulty defecating.

During a vacation to the Jersey Shore in the summer of 2001, Bob McCullough was no longer able to hide his symptoms. Said his lifelong best friend, Scott Geiger of Perkasie: "He just wasn't his normal self. I knew something was not right with him."

"He discovered blood in his stool, and that's when he finally called the doctor," his wife said. By then it was too late. Doctors discovered a massive tumor in his colon. And when they operated to remove it, they found the cancer had spread throughout his liver. "They told us basically it was the worst-case scenario," McCullough said.

When the couple went to the American Cancer Society's Web site (www.cancer.org), they realized the bitter consequences of Bob's silence. When detected early, colorectal cancer is eminently treatable, with a 90 percent five-year survival rate. Yet fewer than four in ten cases are detected early, while still localized. Once the cancer spreads beyond the bowels, the survival rate plummets to just 9 percent.

An Untimely Death

Despite barrages of chemotherapy, the cancer spread to McCullough's spine. On June 25, he died at home, surrounded by his family—one of 56,100 American men and women (in roughly equal numbers) expected to die of colorectal cancer this year. He was forty-eight.

Not quite four months later, his widow has decided to channel her grief into a campaign to educate anyone who will listen about colon cancer. This past weekend, she and more than two dozen friends and relatives joined the national Colon Cancer March on Washington to raise money and awareness.

Her main message echoes the advice of the American Cancer Society and the Colon Cancer Alliance (www.ccalliance.org): If you are fifty or older, insist that your doctor regularly screen you for precancerous polyps. She said doctors estimated that her husband had the polyps for five to seven years before they turned malignant.

She is hoping one widow's frank talk will spare another family what hers has endured. "My kids have lost their father; I have lost my husband," she said. "I don't want anyone else to go through what we've gone through."

Already, she feels, her husband's death was not in vain. After he was diagnosed, all six of his siblings went in for colonoscopies, and five of them discovered precancerous polyps, which were removed, eliminating the risk.

"In a way," his widow said, pausing to look at her husband's photo on the dining-room table, "Bob saved their lives."

Now she hopes to save yours and mine as well.

We Have No Duty to Indulge Bigots

The caller, a middle-aged man, wanted me to know just how upset he was by what happened last month at Abington Memorial Hospital.

The husband of a maternity patient had demanded that only white staffers be allowed to participate in the delivery of the couple's baby—and hospital administrators, to avoid an ugly scene, had acquiesced.

It had upset me, too, I replied.

People have rights in this country, he said.

They sure do, I answered.

No one should be discriminated against, the caller said.

Of course not, I said.

To not honor this white couple's wishes, he said, would be to discriminate against them, to deny them their basic rights to quality medical care.

Uh, say what?

The hospital has a nondiscrimination policy, he pointed out. That means they can't discriminate against white people any more than people of color.

As it turns out, my caller was not at all upset that the hospital had coddled the husband's racism. What upset him was the fact that it later strongly disavowed the decision, after the *Inquirer* made it public, and disciplined the supervisors involved. He was particularly rankled by Abington Memorial president Richard L. Jones Jr., who called the whites-only care afforded the couple "morally reprehensible."

Few things in life are absolute. But this issue of black-and-white is absolutely black and white.

Wrong in Many Ways

Jones, however belatedly, got it right. Morally reprehensible, indeed. My caller, and the bigot he defended, had it so wrong in so many ways.

In the twenty-first century, one would hope that society has moved past such obvious and ugly issues of race. And I believe most of us have.

But here we are in 2003 in one of the nation's largest and most diverse metropolitan areas with attitudes right out of Mississippi 1959; here we are with a modern, well-regarded hospital accommodating those attitudes so as not to ruffle feathers.

And here we are with a phone caller, who on first blush sounds quite reasonable, spewing the shopworn whites-deserve-rights-too argument. As if the downtrodden, oppressed white population of this country, with its 75 percent majority, is about to be marginalized into oblivion. Please.

New century; same old issues.

My phone caller's tortured logic aside, the white couple were never even close to being discriminated against. They had access to the same quality care afforded any patient; they simply did not like the complexion of those serving it up.

Nowhere in the Constitution does it say bigots have the right to demand the rest of us indulge their prejudices.

If the couple were so hell-bent on not having people of color involved in the birth of their baby, they were free to seek out a hospital in, say, northern Idaho instead of choosing Abington, where minorities make up nearly a quarter of the staff. They could have engaged the services of a white midwife.

No, they wanted it both ways.

Accommodating Hatred

The real damaged parties here—the ones who were discriminated against—were the hospital's nonwhite staffers. By the hospital accommodating this ridiculous request worthy of apartheid-era South Africa, it legitimized the racism and sent a message to those employees that they were something less than equal. It also violated the 1964 Civil Rights Act and the hospital's own policies.

But it's nothing personal, guys. I'm sure you can understand. We were just trying to avoid a confrontation.

Of the many lessons to come out of the civil-rights movement, one of the most important was that change does not come by avoiding confrontation.

To accommodate prejudice, even with benign intent, is to perpetuate it.

The next time our favorite Aryan couple find themselves in the family way and looking for medical attention, I hope Abington Memorial will have learned its lesson. The proper response to demands for racial purity is as simple as this: "If you don't like the color of our faces, you're welcome to take your business elsewhere."

Or put another way: "Best of luck delivering in the parking lot."

A Pain That Can't Ever Be Cured

A decade has slipped past like one long moonless night, and still there is no dawn, no end in sight.

The pain is different now from what it was right after the murders, Janice and Gary Benson tell you, less searing, more of a dull, background ache. It is there through meals and chores and daily routines, refusing to leave.

Their son Bryan would be thirty now. Sitting in their home in Warminster, the couple are laughing one minute, telling you what a lovable slob he was, the kid with the world's messiest room. The next, both are in tears, describing the worst moment of this worst of all nightmares: having to tell their two other sons that their brother had been killed.

Can a parent ever move on from the murder of a child? As the Bensons approach the tenth anniversary of Bryan's still-unsolved murder, they can say with an authority they wish was not theirs: No, never.

"And if you could," the mother asks, "what kind of a parent would you be?"

At her Upper Bucks horse farm several miles away, Bonnie Youngers describes almost the exact same lingering pain. Her son, Seann Campbell, died alongside Benson on November 10, 1993, when both were twenty years old. "It's my first thought in the morning and the last thought before I go to bed at night," she says. "It's with me all day, every day."

Stabbings in Suburbia

The two men worked at a West Coast Video store on County Line Road in Warminster, just a few blocks from the neighborhood where both lived with their parents. Some time around closing, an assailant with a knife confronted them. Their bodies, with multiple stab wounds, were found in a back room the next morning. Money was taken—$275—and police suspected a robbery gone awry.

"These were two kids who never did anything to anybody," Gary Benson says, the anger still thick in his throat.

For a while, the story dominated the news. The community rallied, raising $50,000 in reward money. Blue ribbons went up around town. Police interviewed hundreds of people, vainly looking for clues. They successfully extracted a DNA sample from blood and tissue on an earring that possibly was ripped from the assailant during the struggle, but, to date, they have been unable to match it to anyone.

Today, the ribbons are gone, the newspaper clippings yellowed. The reward money sits in a bank, waiting for someone to come forward. Warminster Township Police Detective Scott Selisker says the investigation remains open, but he concedes he needs a break in the case. "There's not a cop in this county that doesn't want to see this crime solved," he said. He asks anyone with information to call him at 215-443-5000.

"You want to know who did it and you want to know why," Youngers says. "Was it for money? Was it for kicks? What would possibly motivate somebody to brutally murder two fine young men? I have made myself ill thinking of all the scenarios. Unfortunately, we just don't know. Everywhere we go, there are no answers."

Otherwise, life has moved forward.

Finding No Peace

The Bensons have a granddaughter now, and they've started a scrapbook so she'll know something about her uncle. Youngers pours her energy into her daughter, Lane, who was twelve when her brother was killed.

Holidays, they agree, are the hardest. All Youngers can think about is how Seann loved to decorate the tree.

"Everyone wants you to get over it," Janice Benson says. She has come to hate the word *closure*.

"There's no such thing as closure," she says. "I could scream at closure. How do you close the fact that your child was murdered? How do you get over that?"

She leads you up the stairs and into a small bedroom—Bryan's room, virtually untouched since his death. Same linens on the bed, same posters on the wall. She opens the closet, and his clothes are there, too. "This was his favorite jacket," she says, holding it to her as only a mother could.

Similarly, Youngers likes to slip into her son's leather jacket. "It's like somehow he's still close," she says.

The parents wait for justice. But they have given up waiting for peace.

"It's like a nightmare that there's no waking from," Youngers says. "Morning comes, and it's still with you."

Two Hundred Years of Life, Two Minutes of Fury

Life lately has been a series of shocks for Jean Knapp.

The first shock came at 7:25 A.M. Tuesday, when the loud crack of breaking trees jolted the Narberth woman from sleep.

The second shock came two minutes later, after the tornado that roared through her wooded acre had passed. She rushed outside, and where native oaks, poplars, and beeches, some two hundred years old, had once towered, she found nothing but devastation. Fallen trees lay everywhere, splintered like toothpicks.

The third shock came later that morning when her longtime arborist, Ken LeRoy of McFarland Tree Service in Philadelphia, arrived. He looked at the tangled mess—shattered branches and limbs literally carpeting the property, chest-deep—and threw out a rough number: $100,000.

Knapp, a quiet, gray-haired woman who is head librarian at Bala Cynwyd Library, was aghast. She could only dream of that kind of money.

LeRoy later clarified. The $100,000 figure was not the cost to remove the debris. It was the approximate value of the dozen or so lost trees, based on industry standards that consider the trees' size, type, and health.

Then came the fourth shock. The cleanup, LeRoy estimated, would cost $40,000 to $50,000—and that did not include planting new trees. A second arborist, John Cox, who runs a tree service in Narberth, thought the cleanup could be done for closer to $30,000.

Insurance No Help

Either way, it was more money than the librarian had. Thank goodness for home insurance, she thought.

The fifth shock came when the insurance adjuster arrived. He'd pay to fix the roof and gutters and replace the shattered picnic table and fence. But as for all those fallen trees, he told her, she was on her own.

Late last week I found Knapp at home in her backyard amid the devastation. She had no idea how to pay for the cleanup or even where to begin.

"Who would ever think of a tornado in Narberth," she said.

And that's when she described the biggest and most profound shock of them all—a shock that, rather than dissipating, has grown with each passing day. It's the shock of loss, the ache of grief, so real she can taste it. Knapp does not have children, but these trees, wiped out in 120 seconds, came close.

You see, she explained, they had been part of her family from the start.

When Knapp's grandparents bought the parcel in 1907, the trees already were mature, old photos show. Her mother grew up there beneath the trees, and so did she and her sister. When Knapp's parents died in the 1980s, the home became hers.

"Except when I was at college, this is the only place I've ever lived," she said.

Bearing Mighty Witness

The trees were always there—for first steps and birthdays and graduations. To simply lie beneath and stare up into. The lumbering giants cooled the property in summer, carpeted it gold in fall, framed winter's fresh snowfalls, and hosted spring's robins.

"That's what really gets me," Knapp said. "When I look out the window now, there's nothing there."

She told me she has not cried since the big trees came down, but as she described them to me, she looked close to doing so. "It makes me very sad," she said. "It took 150 years for those trees to become what they were."

Last week, for the first time in her life, she felt the heat of the afternoon sun beating through her windows.

Soon the chain saws will buzz, and Knapp will find a way to pay the bill. She tries to find the silver lining. After a lifetime of shade gardening, she finally will be able to grow those sun-loving flowers she's long coveted.

But she will miss her old friends—friends that were present for her mother's birth and her own, that watched girls grow into women and women grow old.

In an unpredictable, ever-changing world, the trees whispered of permanence and stability. Their deep roots anchored a family. Now, in death, they speak of life's finiteness and thus, its preciousness.

And in the spring, when the sun again finds the earth and long-dormant seeds sprout new life, they will speak of rebirth as well.

Letting Go of the One That Got Away

Regrets. Every life has them, some more than others. Lately, I have had just one: the home that got away.

I saw it on my first day of house hunting in southeastern Pennsylvania, stumbling serendipitously upon it as if led by divine compass. I took a wrong turn and then another, and soon I was hopelessly lost on a stripe-less country lane. I followed the lane down a steep hill and through a stand of hardwoods.

And there it was.

Standing close against the trees in a meadow that hadn't been mowed, its limestone walls glowing in the morning sun—an 1840s farmhouse. A glorious, lovely farmhouse with deep windowsills, a slate roof, and a porch from which you could imagine the original owners waving farewell as their sons trudged off to defend the Union.

It sat on five rolling acres with a spring and a view. And there was a for-sale sign out front. Gulp!

This was the place my wife and I had dreamed of. The garden could go here, the chicken coop there. Best of all, a tiny stone cottage, which I later learned was the original homestead, still stood on the edge of the property—a writing studio waiting to happen.

I was soon back with my wife and a real estate agent. She pushed open the front door, and our hearts sank.

The Money Pit

Walls were caved in. Floors scarred. Ceilings buckled. Loose wiring hung from the rafters. The kitchen was missing in action. A hot plate and dirty dishes on the toilet told us where the cooking now was done.

Suddenly I knew why the house was in our price range. Everywhere we looked we saw work—and bills. The plumbing, the wiring, the plaster, the chimney, the heating, the cellar all required overhauls. Tens of thousands of dollars were needed just to make it habitable, and tens of thousands more—and hundreds of hours of our time—if it were to ever reclaim its charm.

And still, after a brief ashen silence, my wife and I began plotting.

"This wall could come out," I said.

"The kitchen could go here," she said.

Our agent stood quietly. She had seen it all before. The young couples with big dreams and the way these stone seductresses lured them in, chewed them up, and spat them out, broke and broken.

Finally, she frowned and said: "You have three young children and a new job. In good conscience, I cannot let you buy this place." She knew the score. We could barely afford the asking price, let alone the needed renovations. And I wasn't exactly Bob Vila.

Still, we dithered. We agonized. We wrote up a five-year work plan. In the end, we followed our agent's advice and bought a sensible, suburban two-story with maintenance-free vinyl siding and a new furnace.

And lived happily ever after. Well, almost. It was just our luck that we became close friends with the people next door to the old farmhouse. Every time we visited, we were reminded of our choice. For months, the house stood empty, and we felt only relief. We congratulated ourselves for not stumbling into that sorry quagmire.

A Vision Realized

But then a young couple bought the place and began doing everything we had dreamed of doing. They mowed down the weeds, raised a barn, dug a pond, erected a split-rail fence.

Then one day at dinner at our friends', we met them. And they invited us over to see the inside. We could not believe it was the same house. Walls had been moved, the plaster repaired and painted, the plank floors refinished, a new kitchen installed.

We gushed about the wonderful job they had done. But I saw it behind my wife's smile, and she saw it behind mine. Inside, we were aching.

It was our house just as we had imagined it. But it wasn't ours. It was the one we let get away. Regrets.

I wanted to begrudge this couple their trophy. Quite honestly, I wanted to hate them. But they were much too nice for that. I had to admit they possessed what I did not: the energy, skill, creativity and, most important, faith in their vision to pull it off.

Yes, and the money, too.

Where I saw nothing but heartache, they saw limitless potential.

They deserve their trophy manor. And I'm learning to love my consolation prize, vinyl siding and all.

A Time-Traveling Festival of Folkies

Ever since I was in high school, banging out three-chord Woody Guthrie songs on a secondhand guitar, I have wanted to attend the fabled Philadelphia Folk Festival.

This weekend I finally got my chance. And what a trip it was.

Who said the times they are a-changin'? From the moment I stepped off the yellow school bus into a sea of tie-dyed shirts and patchouli oil on Old Pool Farm near Schwenksville, I was locked in a time warp. Goodbye, 2003. Hello, 1967.

Where have all the folkies gone, long time passing? I just found out.

I knew these people. I had sat next to them at that Crosby, Stills, Nash, and Young concert in Toronto back in 1974. I had rushed the stage with them when Bob Dylan played the Michigan Arena in Ann Arbor a year or two before that. I had camped out in a parking lot with them to snag Joni Mitchell tickets and share communal goatskins of wine.

The only difference was we were now no longer kids. Gray had crept into our beards and ponytails. Paunches had settled into our waistlines and wrinkles into our brows. Bones had grown creaky, and getting up off the damp grass had become more difficult. I spotted more than a few graying longhairs in headbands and orthopedic shoes. Forget the bong. Who brought the Bengay?

A Vision from the Past

I was barely in the front gate when, good Lord, there in front of me, looming like an apparition, was David Crosby himself. Or at least he was a dead ringer for the folk-rock legend, complete with walrus mustache and wild gray locks beneath a balding top.

"Howdy, brother," he said.

Brother? The last time someone other than a sibling called me brother, I was hitching a ride to Boston in a Volkswagen microbus. Can you dig it?

The aging hippies were everywhere—chowing down at the vegetarian food bar; browsing the Guatemalan weavings and earthenware; lounging on straw mats in the damp grass.

Some appeared to be poseurs who traded in their golf shirts for a still-creased tie-dyed frock special ordered from one of those catalogs that cater to nostalgic boomers. But most had the authenticity of people reenacting their history, dressed in their vintage floppy leather hats, calico dresses, red bandannas, and faded overalls.

You got the impression that they had dug through their closets and somehow found the very same duds they had worn to that student sit-in on campus thirty-five years ago.

So what if nothing quite fit anymore? They were letting it all hang out—and I mean that in the most literal sense. The last time I saw this many tattoos, I was at a state prison.

One man paraded around with battery-operated lights blinking in his flowing white beard. Another wore a full-length muslin skirt. Several promenaded in kilts. Boy, did I feel like a dork in my polo shirt and khakis.

The Next Generation

All these aging folkies might give the impression that folk music, if not dead, is on its last legs. But joining the older generation was a whole new legion of tie-dyed, ponytailed, patchouli-scented folkies. They were in their teens and early twenties. They carried guitars and banjos and huddled in circles, strumming songs written before they were born. They danced in the meadow to folk legends old enough to be their grandparents.

They held the promise of renewal. The next generation of folk enthusiasts, reporting for duty, sir.

Before the main acts began Friday evening, the sky darkened ominously and lightning flashed. Kumbaya, my Lord, a hard rain was gonna fall.

And fall it did with a fury that sent old and young alike bolting for shelter. Strangers huddled tightly beneath tarps and overhangs. They flinched in unison as thunder boomed.

And when the rain stopped and music started, the two generations pranced out into the mud together to stomp and frolic and play, their age differences blurred in the muggy twilight. A regular Woodstock moment.

The Philadelphia Folk Festival has been chugging along for forty-two years now. From the looks of things this weekend, my guess is it's good for another forty-two.

Now if I can just get my old bell bottoms zipped, I'll be set for next year.

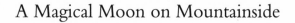

A Magical Moon on Mountainside

"You're going to do WHAT?" I asked.

Allen Male, a retired engineer turned avid mountain trekker, repeated the proposition. He and other members of the Delaware Valley chapter of the Appalachian Mountain Club planned to climb a thousand feet up a mountainside at sunset, perch on a rock ledge, wait for the full moon to rise, and then climb back down.

In the dark.

The Pennsylvania stretch of the Maine-to-Georgia Appalachian Trail is notorious for its rough, jagged, boulder-strewn terrain. Navigating it in daylight is tricky enough, but at night? The plan seemed audacious, reckless, crazy.

"Count me in," I said.

Our leader was Peter Jarrett, a seventh-grade science teacher and running coach in Quakertown, who warned in his e-mail to other mountain-club members: "Please keep in mind that this hike is definitely NOT for the first-time night hiker."

Uh, that would be me. What was I getting myself into?

A few hours before sunset last Tuesday, we met at a trailhead in northern Berks County. The Delaware Valley chapter of the club (www.amcdv.org) has more than five thousand members in Pennsylvania, New Jersey, and Delaware. For this nighttime adventure, just five hardy souls showed up.

Up to the Pinnacle

Joining Jarrett, Male, and me were two veteran marathon runners, Rita Bracken of Easton and Ron Kunkel, who lives on a farm in Berks County.

Of course, I have competed in my share of marathons, too; the only difference was all of mine involved large quantities of beer and chicken wings.

You could say I was intimidated.

Jarrett gathered us in a circle and asked, somewhat ominously, I thought: "Does everyone have water? Does everyone have a flashlight?"

And with that, we set off at a brisk pace. Our destination was a giant rock outcropping known as the Pinnacle, which juts 1,635 feet into the sky and offers one of the most spectacular views anywhere in Pennsylvania.

At first the trail was wide and flat. A piece of cake, I thought. But soon it turned steeply upward. Within minutes all of us were drenched in sweat.

The farther we climbed, the narrower and steeper the trail became until it was nothing but a series of boulders.

The climb took two and a half arduous hours and included an up-close encounter with three beautiful and venomous copperhead snakes.

At a few minutes before the 8:02 P.M. sunset, we saw pink sky through the tree canopy, and soon we stepped out onto a massive rock shelf.

Below us spread a breathtaking quilt-work of farmland and forests.

The Pinnacle was ours.

Waiting for the Moon

We spread out on the warm rocks, pulled sandwiches from our packs, and waited for the 8:49 P.M. moonrise. Kunkel, an astronomy buff, used a sky map and compass to pinpoint where it would break the eastern horizon. "And Mars should rise right about there," he said, pointing.

As darkness settled in, a cool breeze washed over us. A screech owl called. In the valley below, farmhouses lit up one by one like tiny stars.

I inched back from the ledge. How, I wondered, were we ever going to get down from here? Jarrett, who has led a dozen of these moonlight climbs over the last three years, put my mind to ease. He would lead us back by an old fire trail with few hazards.

We checked our watches. Moonrise had come and gone with no moon. The thick haze, it seemed, had swallowed it whole.

"I don't think we're going to see it," a disappointed Male said.

At 9:15, just as we were about to give up, Jarrett yelled, "There it is!" A giant, dusty red ball broke through the clouds, bathing us in a soft light.

We lingered a half hour longer. Then, flashlights in hand, we began a slow, careful—and uneventful—descent.

At the bottom, the trail dumped us beside a large reservoir. As if in salute, our friend the moon tossed a quivering silver beam across the water's surface.

The five of us, sweaty, muddy, and totally content, stood in awed silence, delaying one moment longer our inevitable return to the world beyond.

Phones Driving Us to Distraction

Not long ago, I was a cell-phone virgin. I didn't own one and didn't want one. I had a phone at work and a phone at home, and that was as in touch with the world as I wanted to be.

My idea of getting wired was gulping a double espresso, not signing my life away to Cingular.

In those B.C. (Before Cell) days, I made sport of ridiculing the self-important chatterbox slaves who were convinced the world would stop—screech to a crashing halt—if they were out of touch for one solitary second. I watched them droning on at restaurants, malls, ballgames, picnics—and wondered what on earth they were finding to jabber about.

Now I'm one of them, a cell-phone convert. And I wonder no more. How I ever got along without one of these things I'll never know. Equipped with my mobile communicator, I feel like Spock on a *Star Trek* episode.

But, like almost everyone else who owns a cell phone, I have a problem. I can't resist using mine—to check voice mail, talk with my editors, return messages—as I hurtle down the expressway in a two-ton steel box at frightening speeds.

As though Philadelphia's crowded roads don't have enough headaches already, they've now been invaded by vast armies of mobile goofus gabbers. To which I say: Reporting for duty, sir!

That Vision Thing

My favorite soldiers in this assault are the members of the bifocals brigade (of which I am a recent inductee). You see them swerving at you in traffic, with one hand on the steering wheel, the other hand holding their cell phones out at full arm's length as they squint quizzically at the keypad, trying to read the tiny numbers.

We chatty commuters are checking blind spots, passing, and merging into rush hour—all while yammering away about the minutiae of our lives.

If you see us coming, look out, because we won't be looking out for you.

At least when we run each other off the road, we can dial 911 before the wreckage even comes to rest.

Do you think this is what AT&T had in mind when it told us to reach out and touch someone?

A first-ever study of driving habits by the University of North Carolina paints a sobering picture of how distracted motorists have become. The study videotaped drivers in metro Philadelphia and in North Carolina and found that 30 percent talked on cell phones as they drove. The average driver took thirteen seconds to dial a cell phone. At sixty miles per hour, that means the car traveled nearly a quarter mile with the driver looking down at the phone. Oh my.

The study found that 40 percent of drivers read or write behind the wheel, usually while stopped. What is this, community college?

An additional 46 percent groom themselves as they drive, and a whopping 71 percent bring new meaning to the term *fast food*, eating or drinking as they zoom along. Rule me guilty on that last count. If I add any more selections to my front-seat buffet, I'll need a lunch-wagon license.

A Close Shave

In my daily commutes, I've seen it all: Women applying makeup; men using electric shavers; couples mashing.

I even know a guy who claims to play guitar while driving. You will note that a guitar requires two hands to play, which leaves approximately no hands to steer with. In his own defense, my friend says he serenades the dashboard only while cruising down lonely stretches of road. Well, why didn't you say so, Elvis?

All this distraction comes at a cost to human safety. As the *Inquirer*'s Marian Uhlman reported last week, it is to blame for roughly a quarter of all car accidents, according to National Highway Traffic Safety Administration estimates.

That's a lot of distraction.

I must confess, since getting my cell phone, I sometimes glance up mid-conversation and have no idea how I got where I am. One second I'm in Baltimore, the next I'm entering Chester. Hey, what happened to Delaware?

So, my fellow crazed commuters, whaddaya say? Shall we try regulating ourselves before the government kindly does it for us?

Here's a place to start: I promise not to call you from the road if you promise not to call me.

<!-- decorative flourish -->

Gravestones Tell Stories of the Past

Sunrise is still an hour off, and I should be asleep, not standing amid the gravestones and heartbreak of this old cemetery, beckoning those who settled this land I now call home.

Something had awakened me. What was it? A truck's backfire? The drill of a woodpecker? And I slipped silently from bed, out the front door into the purple-streaked stillness of dawn.

I began walking—out of the subdivision where farmers once plowed, down one wooded hill and up the next. At the top was a cemetery beside a white church.

The gate was open. I turned in.

And now I linger in the half-light with the remains of those who came to these hills before me. They were German immigrants who cleared the land, planted crops, and survived by their own making. For more than two hundred years they lived and died here.

The oldest grave I find belongs to a Revolutionary War veteran, Private Peter Engleman, who died in 1812 at age sixty. There are others who lived even longer. Esther Funk, born in 1821, lived eighty-six years. Anna Weider, born in 1815, lived to ninety-one.

But most were less fortunate.

The carved stones tell of hard lives and sudden deaths, of war and accidents, of disease and sickness. They tell of family losses that today would be considered unbearable.

Each stone tells a story, and the smallest stones tell the saddest stories of all. They belong to the babies.

Dozens of them line the ground.

Nine Births, Nine Deaths

There are the Diehl children. Nine tiny stones. Isena made it to thirteen; Ursula and Alma to five; Alfred to four. Golden and Loftin and Urban and Ottis and Erma, all gone before age two.

You picture the parents and try to imagine their grief, but it is unimaginable. Nine children. Nine tiny stones.

There are the Fries children. Ida was three when she was taken in 1887. Two years later, the twins, Samuel and Charles, survived just fourteen days. And two years after that came Annie, who died with her twenty-seven-year-old mother in the summer of 1891.

And the father, Charles, this poor soul who lost all his children and his wife, how did he go on? Somehow he found a way, living to be eighty-four.

The gravestones measure lives in precious months and days.

There are the Reichenbach children: Charles, sixteen years, four months, eight days; William, one month, four days; Harvey, twenty-nine days.

There are the Shifferts: Beulah, eleven years, twenty-four days; Charles, ten years, four months, twenty-eight days; and little Cora, one year, nine months, twenty-two days.

The tiniest tombstones have no names. One simply reads, "Our Baby." Another, "Our Infant." One bears the inscription: "Asleep With Jesus."

There in the cool morning, you can almost see the tiny coffins and the sturdy German farmers gathered on this hilltop to lower their newborns into the ground. You can almost hear the prayers and the hymns sung to no music. Almost begin to understand the steely, stoic resolve to carry on.

A Soldier's Story

You stop at the family plot of William and Maria Ruth, who brought four children into this world—and soon lost three of them. But the fourth, a boy named for his father, survived and grew strong—and left this hill to go fight in World War I. His gravestone, decorated with a large star and the proud words "Our Son," tells the story: "Died in France, July 31, 1918. Age twenty years, five months, thirteen days."

As the sun rises, it's as if the ghosts have risen with it to whisper the past to you, to tell a newcomer the secrets this piece of earth holds.

The voices speak of a time before hospitals and ambulances and vaccines. They talk of love and loss, of pride and humility, of joy and grief.

The sun breaks over the trees, bathing the white church in a brilliant glow. It's time to head back. I scan the graves a last time and say a silent farewell to the pioneers who tamed this land, to the mothers who died in childbirth, to the newborns who never saw their first birthday.

I pause over the nine tiny stones of the Diehl children and at the foot of Colonel William Ruth. I want them all to know that their stone-carved stories are not forgotten. Then I turn through the gate and down the hill, the rising sun warm on my neck.

A Bypassed and Bygone Life

On Sunday, my wife and I loaded our children into the car and went in search of the other Pennsylvania—the one far from the concrete city and vinyl-sided suburbs. The one still not colonized by chain restaurants, multiplexes, and convenience stores.

We found it in the shadow of the Appalachian Mountains amid the undulating gold-and-green farmland of northwest Berks County. At a place called Haag's Hotel.

For nearly two hundred years, the hotel has held court in the one-street village of Shartlesville, which for decades hugged the main drag between Newark, New Jersey, and Cincinnati.

The hotel thrived on the constant stream of travelers, lodging the weary and dishing up vast quantities of traditional Pennsylvania Dutch cuisine.

When the hotel burned to the ground in 1914, Albert Haag rebuilt it—and there it stands today, now run by his grandson and three great-grandchildren.

It is a place caught in time.

In front of the stone-pillared porch, the original gas pump, long out of service, still stands, and rustic chairs fashioned from tree branches beckon.

Inside, you get the sense that not so much as a teacup has changed in the last fifty years. The floor is worn. The bubbled varnish on the wood beams has blackened with age.

No One Leaves Hungry

My family takes a table beneath a portrait of George Washington, and Courtney, our teenage waitress who lives across the street, begins filling the table with dishes of food until there is room for no more.

The platters are piled with fried chicken, ham, sausages, sweet potatoes, mashed potatoes, dried corn, cabbage, applesauce, green beans, baked beans, pudding, and more.

It's an obscenity of food. Simple, no-nonsense, stick-to-your-ribs food. And if you manage to finish it, the staff brings more, just as it has always done.

John Seitzinger, who still speaks the Pennsylvania Dutch dialect of German with other old-timers in town, is the current owner. He was born in one of the inn's eight guestrooms in 1929 and remembers the heyday.

"It was a busy road," he told me, speaking of old U.S. Route 22, now a sleepy lane. "The large trucks would come through. The Greyhound bus had a stop at Haag's Hotel."

On weekends, as many as thirty tour buses a day stopped. The hotel could seat three hundred, and there was often a waiting list for dinner, he said.

The waiting lists are now history. On my visit, just four families shared the cavernous hall.

There once were five gas stations, two mechanic garages, a pharmacy and three grocery stores in town, all now long gone.

Seitzinger remembers the exact day when everything changed.

"The Interstate [I-78] came in and bypassed our village in November 1956," he said. Almost overnight, the crowds stopped coming.

End of an Era

For several years, tour buses continued to call, but by the early 1970s, they, too, had largely evaporated.

"A lot of businesses shut down," Seitzinger's son, Ashley Seitzinger, working behind the hotel's bar, said. "The traffic just didn't come through town anymore."

It was a story played out in thousands of small cities across America. Here in Shartlesville, population 450, the effect was to freeze the past like a hand-colored photograph.

Standing in the middle of Main Street—and you can do so without fear of being run over—it's easy to imagine what America was like in that simpler time before highways and television and big-box chain stores.

After homemade pie and ice cream, we stroll the four-block village. Fire Chief Gene Spotts, who has lived here since birth, walks out to welcome us.

He remembers when the streets were so crowded he could make good money selling Kool-Aid. Now a single family on the street draws attention.

Later, the senior Seitzinger acknowledges that the family hotel today barely breaks even. And he laments that his grandchildren are choosing to leave town for careers of their own.

Yet he holds hope for the future. As he proudly tells me, "We had our first great-grandchild on Friday. He's the seventh generation."

Hand Woodwork Is His Simple Joy

Al Gerhards stands in his shady backyard near Downingtown
and sights down a short length of oak he has just split from a
log plucked from the woods behind his home.

This piece will do.

Straddling a sawhorse-like bench that looks as if it belongs in
a medieval village, he wedges the slab of oak in a viselike contraption and applies pressure with a crude but ingenious foot
pedal to lock it in place.

Then he goes to work.

Using a large, razor-sharp drawknife that looks like a museum piece—and is in fact about a hundred years old—he begins shaving the raw wood. First he squares and sizes the four
sides, using a pair of tarnished calipers to ensure accuracy.
Then he begins rounding the edges.

The wood is green and supple, and as he works the curled
shavings pile at his feet. Soon you see what he is up to. The
piece is being shaped, slowly, meticulously, into a slender chair
rail.

"This is the way they did it in the old days," he tells you.
The very old days. The days of knights and armor and castles.

Gerhards, sixty-three, who emigrated from Germany when
he was a child, has done research, and many of the tools he
uses today were in use as early as the thirteenth century in Eu-
rope. The bench he works on—known as a shaving horse or
schnitzelbank in German—has origins even farther back.

The early arrivals to this country brought their tools and skills along, using them to build cabins and barns, rocking chairs and cribs, pitchforks and hay rakes.

"Sitting here," he says as he works, birds singing and squirrels scampering overhead, "I can just visualize the settlers doing this kind of work."

When the chair is completed, he will gather cattail leaves from the banks of the Brandywine River and use them to weave the rush seat. Gerhards' self-appointed mission is to keep this dying art—known as green woodworking because, unlike conventional cabinetry, the lumber is not dried first—alive.

In a modern, climate-controlled age of computer dating and microwave dinners, Gerhards embraces a simple life now all but forgotten.

He earns his living making dental crowns and bridges in West Chester. Each evening, however, he retreats to his garage or to a cool spot beneath a shade tree to whittle and carve and shape logs into graceful chairs and tools. Several times a year, he gives demonstrations at folk festivals.

He sells twenty to thirty pieces a year, everything from steam-bent pitchforks he can make in five or six hours to rocking chairs that take him weeks to finish. "It's fun to do, but you can't retire on it," he says.

A former world champion boomerang-thrower who is naturally talented with his hands, Gerhards became smitten by old-time woodworking when he stumbled on *The Woodwright's Shop* on PBS some twenty years ago. He hunted out traditional tools at flea markets and began to experiment.

The only power tool he uses is a chain saw to cut tree trunks to length. He chooses trees that are diseased or have been damaged by lightning or windstorms. White oak, with its tight grain pattern, is his favorite. From there, he uses steel wedges and a mallet to split them to size.

He pauses from his work to run his hand over the emerging spindle he is shaping. "There are no splinters because I'm always following the grain of the wood," he says.

It's a rule that applies to other aspects of his life, as well. Go with the grain. Learn from your forebears. Appreciate the past to better live the present. Understand the rules of nature and follow them.

Do these things and life's voyage will be smooth and satisfying.

Gerhards, a serious man of few words, swears the wood speaks to him. Then cracking a grin, he deadpans, "I finally figured out what it was saying: 'Don't quit your day job.'"

For the moment, he won't. But in his heart and in his dreams, he already is centuries away.

In Healing, Reminder of Life's Final Hurt

As dozens of my colleagues hunkered down with American troops in the Iraqi desert, I was embedded in a life-and-death struggle of an entirely different kind.

My post was a Bucks County nursing home, and the war I witnessed over a six-week period was against that insidious enemy known as age.

Let me tell you, like all wars, this one is hell.

What brought me to the nursing home was not journalistic curiosity but medical necessity. Two herniated disks in my neck sent me in search of a physical therapist. I found a good one who practiced in rented space in the nursing home's basement right beside a small beauty parlor where, each morning, old women caused a traffic jam of wheelchairs as they maneuvered to have their hair set.

Three mornings a week, I arrived for traction and exercise. Several of my fellow patients were just like me, in the words of the physical therapist, "forty-something guys who still think they're twenty." Middle-aged men who stupidly overdid it and hurt themselves.

Yep, that would be me.

But we were the clear minority. Most of the therapist's patients were residents from upstairs. Starting at 8:30 each morning, attendants in bright floral smocks would begin arriving with them. Some came with canes, some with walkers. Most arrived in wheelchairs.

They were stiff and weak and achy—and very old, in the final pages of the long books that are their lives. The physical therapist wasn't pretending to fix them. His job was simply to help them make it through each remaining day a little more comfortably.

Over the weeks, I got to know several of them and the world they inhabit. It is a world most of us breeze past unnoticed as we go about our lives. A world of empty hours and countless days, not unpleasant but without future, where the only checkout is death.

There was Anna, a birdlike woman with a thin wisp of white hair, who rolled in with her arm in a sling from a fall. The therapist and his twenty-four-year-old assistant tried to engage her, get her to do a few light exercises. She would have nothing to do with it.

"Why am I here?" she asked.

"We're going to work on that arm," he said.

"Why can't I hear what you say?"

The therapist let the question slide, but she asked it again, this time more urgently. He knelt before her, his face close to hers, and said loudly but gently, "I think it's age-related, Anna."

There was chubby, cheery Sue, who each morning lay on a low table, struggling to lift her hips a few inches into the air. One day, she smiled sweetly at me and volunteered: "My mother always told me, 'Never get old.'" Then she paused, and the smile slipped from her lips. Somehow it hadn't worked out that way.

Across the room was Doris, hooked to an oxygen tank and dressed improbably in purple high heels. Her mission was to get out of her wheelchair without help. She rocked to build momentum. "One, two, three. Up you go," the assistant coached cheerfully. Doris tried, and tried again.

"I just can't do it," she said.

And, saddest of all, there was Violet, who by all appearances had given up. Her job was to tug a rope through a pulley. But she just let the braided cord slip from her lifeless hands.

The therapist admonished: "Come on, Violet. What's going on with you? Show me you still have something in your body to work with."

But Violet was done. Checked out. She sat, gazing blankly ahead.

On my last day, I arrived to find the place nearly empty. All of my elderly friends were missing and for a brief, sudden second I was filled with sadness. Had their time come? All at once?

But after a few minutes, in they wandered: Doris, still on her oxygen but this time in more sensible shoes; Anna, her bruises turning yellow; always cheerful Sue; rail-thin Ray. And poor Violet.

As they struggled with their routines, wincing and groaning, the young assistant working the muscles in my neck lowered her lips near my ear and whispered her confession:

"God, I hope I never get old."

* * *

A Slow Response to Toddler's Crisis

One moment, toddler Chetin Atillasoy was resting comfortably on the family-room sofa. The next, his arms were flailing, eyes rolling back in his head, and face turning blue.

In an upscale development in Yardley on June 6, it happened that fast.

The two-year-old boy everyone calls Chewy had been sick with a fever. His mother, Aylin Atillasoy, thirty-seven, who lives with her physician husband and three sons, gave the baby a cool bath and placed him in front of the television to watch cartoons.

He was absorbed in Scooby-Doo, and the mother walked out to the driveway to greet another mother who was dropping off a child for a play date with Atillasoy's oldest son, who is seven.

When she stepped back inside a few minutes later, she found Chewy in the grips of a violent seizure, his body flailing. She grabbed him and raced into the kitchen for the telephone, but it was not in its cradle. In her panic, she could not find it amid papers on the counter.

The mother raced outside, screaming "He's not breathing! Call 911!" That's just what neighbor Aubria Pollazzi, who was outside with her two-year-old daughter, did.

The two women brought the unconscious boy back into the house, laid him on the floor, and began trying to revive him as an operator stayed on the line. "Aylin was frantic. She was paralyzed with panic. It was just horrible," Pollazzi, twenty-nine, said. "I just started going to work on him. I didn't even think about it. He was purple and blue. I felt for a pulse. His heart was racing. I took a big breath and blew into his mouth, but his lungs did not go up."

A Frantic Ten Minutes

The dispatcher told the women to check the boy's air passage. His jaws were clenched shut, and Pollazzi had to pry them apart with both hands. She found his tongue blocking his throat and cleared it. This time her breaths filled his lungs. She continued breathing for him, she estimates, for ten minutes before he began breathing shallowly on his own.

The whole while, the hysterical mother was on the phone with the emergency dispatcher. "I'm sobbing, I'm crying," she said. "I'm screaming, 'Where is the ambulance?' She kept saying, 'Ma'am, calm down. The ambulance is on the way.'"

Neighbors began to gather. A nurse who lives in the neighborhood arrived. A police officer rolled up. But no ambulance. Said Pollazzi: "I know things seem long in a situation like that, but I was pretty calm—and it took forever."

According to the Yardley Makefield Emergency Unit, which dispatched the ambulance, the 911 call came in at 12:55

P.M. and the ambulance arrived at the Atillasoys' home sixteen minutes later, at 1:11 P.M.

"I just assumed they'd be there like lightning, especially when you hear a baby is not breathing," Pollazzi said.

A Question Remains

The good news is that Chewy, who has no history of medical problems, is fine. He was rushed to St. Mary Medical Center in Langhorne, where he regained consciousness and was later released. On a recent morning, he bounced around his house, playing with toys and showing off for a visitor, apparently no worse for his close encounter with death.

Atillasoy said her pediatrician diagnosed a febrile seizure brought on by a fever spike caused by a viral infection.

She is thankful to have her son alive, eternally grateful for her neighbor's levelheaded action. And she's asking, loudly, the question any parent would ask: Is sixteen minutes an acceptable emergency response time when a child has stopped breathing? "It's not like he had a splinter," she said. "How much more serious does it get?"

The delay is particularly perplexing considering that a Yardley Makefield fire station is just 2.2 miles away. On a recent afternoon, the drive took three minutes going the speed limit.

I asked Steve Lehrman, assistant chief of the emergency unit, to answer the Atillasoys' question. He said the response time is being investigated and he will comment when it is completed. I'll let you know what he says.

In the meantime, Aylin Atillasoy has learned an important lesson about self-reliance. She is hosting a refresher cardiopulmonary resuscitation course at her home next week. All the neighbors are invited.

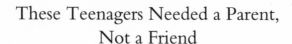

These Teenagers Needed a Parent,
Not a Friend

Dysfunction in all directions.

That was the scene yesterday in a Willow Grove district courtroom where Megan Smith and her eighteen-year-old son, James, appeared together on a variety of charges that can best be summarized like this:

One messed-up family.

If this were a script for a soap opera, it would be rejected as too tawdry, too unbelievable. No parent could get it this wrong, could she?

Megan Smith, dressed in a lavender sweater and pink pants, her makeup meticulously applied, her blond hair falling over her shoulders, stood before the magistrate as a poster child for what happens when adults act like children.

When parents choose popularity over principle.

When a mother exercises the judgment of a preschooler.

As one parent who knows Smith told me later, "Basically, she's a thirty-six-year-old teenager."

Basically, that would be correct.

Smith is charged with corruption of minors and other offenses. She is accused of allowing about twenty-five ninth graders to drink alcohol at her home in December and for helping the teens sneak booze into a New Year's Eve party at a house in Hatboro.

During the December party, a fourteen-year-old girl became extremely drunk, and Smith is accused of escorting the girl into James Smith's bedroom. Now James Smith is charged with deviate sexual intercourse, accused of having sex with the intoxicated minor.

And It Gets Worse

Could this tale possibly get any more trashy? Oh, yes it could.

New charges were filed last week against Smith, accusing her of renting a motel room on three occasions so her fourteen-year-old daughter and the girl's fourteen-year-old boyfriend could sleep together. You've got to give her points for being helpful.

And did I mention she is also charged with using a Web posting to threaten and demean the girl her son is accused of raping?

I, myself, got a taste of the wrath of Supermom. After I wrote about this case, I received an angry voice message from a woman identifying herself as Megan Smith. The message maligned the character of the girl and said not only did I have all my facts wrong, so did the police.

The voice on the other end also said, "I'm about ready to kill you." I'll assume my caller was speaking figuratively. Hello, Mom? Anybody home?

Thursday's hearing was not pretty.

James Smith sat beside his mother, looking scared and shaken. A few feet away, the young girl he is accused of raping sat with her parents, looking just as scared and shaken.

Waiting in a back room, in leg shackles and handcuffs, was the boy who had been involved with Smith's daughter, who was also on hand. He was there to testify about Smith arranging motel rooms for their liaisons.

The reason he was in restraints, according to his mother, Ana Veloz, was that he had violated a no-contact order by visiting Smith's daughter.

A Son Lost

Outside the courtroom, Veloz and her fiancé, Christopher Reinert, spoke bitterly of Smith and how they say she corrupted their son, who ran away from home when they tried to rein in the young love affair.

According to the couple, Smith not only rented motel rooms for the fourteen-year-olds, she gave them alcohol and went behind Veloz's and Reinert's backs to help the boy and girl rendezvous. One time, they said, they found the children necking in the backseat of a car while Megan Smith sat at the wheel.

When they confronted her, she dismissed their concerns, they said. "She kept telling us, 'They're young; they're in love,'" Reinert said.

"I think she should be in jail forever," Veloz said. "The damage she has done to my son, it's unbelievable."

And so goes this twisted, utterly depressing morality tale.

It is a tale about what can happen when adults abdicate the most basic of responsibilities. About the unwritten pact we sign when we bring children into this world, and the young lives we hurt when we break it. About being friends to our children when what they really need are parents.

Parents who provide guidance and structure. Not booze and motel rooms.

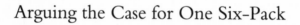

Arguing the Case for One Six-Pack

I'm standing in a beer distributorship in Harleysville, surrounded by enough brew to float the Fifth Fleet, and ask what seems to me a perfectly reasonable question: "Can I buy a six-pack, please?"

The owner doesn't miss a beat.

"Nope," he says, "you can't."

"I can't?"

"You can only buy a case."

"But I don't want a case," I say. "I want a six-pack."

"If you want a six-pack, you need to buy it at a bar."

"Do I need to drink it there?"

"No. You just need to buy it there."

"At a bar?"

"At a bar."

"But I'm here now. And you're a beer store. The sign says 'Cold Beer.' Why do I have to go to a bar?"

The owner sighs deeply as if he's been through this many times before with clueless newcomers to his state. He proceeds to tell me about Pennsylvania's beer laws—specifically, the one that says it's legal to drive off from a beer store with twenty-four cold ones but not with six.

Makes sense to me. If we're going to send drinking drivers onto our roads, the commonwealth wants to make sure they don't run dry.

"Look," he says, "if you want a six-pack, you have to find a bar. Of course, you'll pay a premium for it."

"I'll pay more? For the same beer?"

"Right. It's to keep people from driving around with six-packs."

"But they can drive around with cases of beer?"

He doesn't answer.

Shades of Stalinist Russia

Of Pennsylvania's many silly, archaic laws, this one most deserves the "Ben Must Have Taken a Few Too Many Volts Through the Kite String Award" for mind-frying stupidity.

Pennsylvanians buying beer remind me of those poor Soviets in Stalinist Russia waiting in line in the snow every week to get their state-issued loaf of stale bread.

Comrades! You will buy your state-sanctioned beverages only from the government store, and you will buy them only in the quantities that we tell you to! Is that understood?

We Pennsylvania newcomers, who have tasted the freedom of buying as few beers as we want, find this all immensely amusing. But when I point out the absurdity of it to longtime residents, they look at me like I'm questioning the decision to split from the Crown.

It's insanity. If I want to have beer with a cookout, I cannot buy it at the supermarket where I get the burgers and potato salad. I need to make a special trip to the official beer store, and—under penalty of law—I must load up on vast quantities. And risk a hernia lugging it out to the car.

But have no fear, alcohol abusers. In case you're inconvenienced by all this, our state law has a drink-and-drive loophole just for you.

Cold Suds to Go

All you need to do is drop by any tavern—my guess is you're sitting in one already—and plop down a few bucks more than you'd pay for the same six-pack in New Jersey (which, by the way, has a slightly lower percentage of alcohol-related traffic fatalities than Pennsylvania).

These hard-core drinkers are exactly the ones who will pay any price for a beer—even at the shakedown carryout prices charged by the taverns. Uh, so why again do we have this law?

After I left the beer store empty-handed, I got on the phone with Pennsylvania Liquor Control Board spokeswoman Molly McGowan and asked her to explain the logic. Long pause.

"That's been a law since 1934 or something," she said, "so I'm not sure what the original thinking was."

After checking, she said the law was established on the heels of Prohibition to help put an end to bootlegging. The liquor board has not taken a position on whether the by-the-case law still makes sense sixty years later.

Let me help out here: It doesn't.

It is great news for tavern owners (state-sponsored price gouging), beer distributorships (mandated volume), and drunken drivers (easy takeout access from the same place you've been drinking all night). But for law-abiding citizens who simply want to tip a cold one on the back deck after work without having twenty-three left in the carton?

It's nothing but a hassle.

Our Beloved Guns Kill Our Children

I'm tired.

Tired of children using guns.

To kill one another.

To kill their parents.

To kill their educators.

To kill themselves.

I'm tired and sick and disgusted.

It happened again last week on a spring morning that held nothing but the promise of rejuvenation. It happened, improbably, in the sleepy central Pennsylvania borough of Red Lion, population 6,130.

Red Lion is the kind of place parents will tell you is good for raising kids. The schools have no metal detectors. It's the kind of place—so quaint as to be almost corny—where these things are not supposed to happen.

But it did happen, at 7:38 A.M. Thursday in the crowded cafeteria of the local middle school. Police say eighth grader James Sheets arrived with three loaded handguns in his backpack and fatally shot principal Eugene Segro and then himself.

He was fourteen years old. The guns came not from some shadowy arms merchant but from his stepfather's locked safe. The boy had found the key.

The shooting, while disturbing, was something less than shocking. And that perhaps is the saddest part of all.

A Tragic Precedent

Thursday's double killing came five years to the day after another fourteen-year-old boy shot dead his science teacher at a school dance in Erie County.

It happened just over two years after a fourteen-year-old girl shot and wounded a classmate in the lunchroom of a middle school in Lycoming County.

It happened six months and seventeen days after a twelve-year-old boy walked into his suburban home near Bethlehem in Northampton County and, according to prosecutors who have charged him with homicide, shot his mother point-blank in the face with a rifle taken from his father's gun cabinet.

It happened a decade after a fifteen-year-old boy fatally shot a classmate at Upper Perkiomen High School in Montgomery County.

It happened four years and four days after the event by which America now measures all other student gun violence— the shooting spree at Columbine High School in Littleton, Colorado, which left fifteen dead and nearly two dozen wounded.

Should I continue? The once unthinkable has become terrifyingly close to routine. And our collective response? A sigh. A shake of the head. A shrug. Resignation. More helpless despair than determined resolution.

If foreign terrorists were randomly picking off our children in their school yards, the world's most powerful military would be launching the next invasion. But because the killers are American children, we simply pause to lament the shame of it all.

And then move on.

Angst but No Action

Ultimately, after the hand-wringing subsides, we will do nothing. Because to do something would require us to start with the millions of guns that populate every city block, every small town, every suburban neighborhood in the country.

And that's something Americans are unwilling to do. We cherish our guns, it seems, more than we cherish our children. How did our priorities get this twisted?

The lambs are slaughtering one another with the firepower they are finding in Mom and Dad's bedroom closet. We should be outraged; we should be moved to action. If nothing else, we should agree that children and guns do not belong under the same roof. Instead, we sigh and shake our heads.

And await the next bloodbath.

The few who will dare to question the sanity of this guns-at-all-costs culture will be roundly shouted down by the fierce defenders of Americans' unfettered right to bear arms.

The defenders will say that guns are not the problem. It's society; it's bad parenting; it's dysfunctional homes and fragmented families and disenfranchised youth. Perhaps, but I know this: If a pubescent killer shows up in my child's classroom, I hope to God he's armed with something that takes a little more effort than the squeeze of a trigger.

We Americans love our guns. We've made our bed with them. And now our children must lie in it.

She's an Athlete No One Can Forget

Some moments in life stay with you till your dying day.

For Katie Samson, a gifted athlete who was never very good at sitting still, that moment came on a snowy slope in Radnor on January 29, 2000.

It was a simple, happy moment, one of the thousands that are meant to blend into the stuff of happy youthful memories. It ended up being the turning point of her young life.

Samson, home from Middlebury College in Vermont, was sledding with friends. Her sled hit a bump, sending her airborne. "It was just one of those fluke accidents," she says mat-

ter-of-factly, sitting in her wheelchair on the patio of her Radnor home.

"I kind of landed on my head. As soon as I hit, it broke my
neck, and I was immediately paralyzed."

She remembers the rest of her slide down the hill as a silent,
painless dream. It was almost like floating.

What came next was less ethereal—the weeks in the hospital
followed by months in a rehabilitation center, as she put it,
"figuring out how one lives in a wheelchair."

For this energetic downhill skier and star lacrosse goalie who
helped Middlebury bag a national championship the year before, it was a raw, shattering transition.

She spent several weeks in despair. Then she decided to get
on with life. "I started to rethink everything. I thought, 'This is
something I can actually live with.'" The rest of Samson's story
is an amazing testament to human resiliency and willpower.

Sitting with her in the sun, the first bees of spring bumbling
lazily about us, I am struck by this young woman's profound
lack of self-pity. This is her new life as a paraplegic, motionless
from the chest down. She's conquering it, one obstacle at a
time.

A year after her accident, Samson was back at Middlebury,
where she became a coach for her old lacrosse team. She coun-
seled other young paralysis victims. She taught drama. She
even took a modern dance class, where she could whirl about
and almost forget she was anchored to a steel chair on wheels.

In May, she delivered the commencement address to her
classmates, though she would not graduate herself until the
next semester. In it, she talked of her battle to accept her new
life. "In the end," she told her classmates, "I have so much to
be thankful for. I think we all do."

When her turn to graduate with honors came two months ago, she joined her classmates in skiing down a Vermont mountain in cap and gown. To do it, she mastered a special sitting-ski rig. At the bottom, her family and a throng of supporters cheered her.

"It's one of those moments of my life I'll never forget," she says.

And another unforgettable moment: In December 2001, she wheeled the Olympic torch up Broad Street in Philadelphia on its way to Salt Lake City, her ever-present family and friends applauding her, tears streaming down her freckled cheeks.

Each summer since her accident, Samson has joined a rowing team on the Schuylkill, her hands taped to the oars because they no longer can grip.

Now twenty-three and back home, she is job hunting and preparing for an internship at the Philadelphia Museum of Art. She drives a modified van, and is largely independent, though she needs help getting in and out of bed. Did I mention she is writing a youth novel based on Rembrandt's early years?

But what has been occupying her attention lately is the Third Annual Katie Samson Lacrosse Festival, which will take place Saturday at the Haverford School in Haverford. All proceeds will go to fund spinal-cord-injury research and care.

Meanwhile, the irrepressible Samson keeps dreaming and striving—and proving each day that broken bodies do not need to break spirits. Her long-term goal is to earn a doctoral degree so she can teach at a university.

"And I'm still tying to figure out how I can adapt a lacrosse stick so I can catch and throw," she says. Somehow you know she will find a way.

Odyssey of Mind Is a Trip, All Right

Usually I spend my weekends at home with three noisy, wound-up, bouncing-off-the-wall children. Saturday, I super-sized my order and spent it with a thousand of them from all over southeastern Pennsylvania.

My ears are still ringing.

The event was the regional Odyssey of the Mind competition at Allen High School in Allentown. I was one of the volunteer judges. How do I let myself get talked into these things?

"Bring your Motrin," the competition's regional director, Kathy Young, had warned us at training earlier. "I'll be honest with you: By the end of the day, you'll be a little frazzled."

And she was right. Not that it wasn't a fun and eye-opening experience, watching these young minds charge full steam ahead without constraint.

Odyssey of the Mind is an international competition designed to foster creative teamwork and problem-solving skills in children from kindergarten through high school. The kids, in teams of five to seven, tackle problems such as powering homemade vehicles or building balsa-wood structures that can support hundreds of pounds. They then create a skit, complete with costumes and backdrops, in which to present their solution.

Each team has a coach, usually a parent, but the rules are strict: The kids can receive no hands-on help.

Saturday's twelve-hour creative duke-out determined which teams will advance to the state finals next month.

The Giggle Factor

The kids came from all over the region—from Philadelphia and Yardley, Lansdale and Harleysville, Ambler and Bethlehem. They came in all shapes, sizes, and colors. They had one thing in common: Every last one of them had the wiggles and giggles.

All right, who gave these guys the Oreos and Coke for breakfast?

As a staging-area judge, my job was to calm them down before they performed the skits they had been preparing since October. Yeah, right.

Most of the kids were full of unbridled exuberance. A few were petrified. One little boy looked up at me with big eyes and confessed in a quivering voice, "I'm really nervous."

The only thing I could think to do was the Lamaze breathing I had learned when my wife was expecting our first baby. So there we were, puffing out short, rapid breaths together like a couple in a maternity ward. It must have worked. He got through his performance just fine.

Not all the teams were so lucky. One built its prop about an inch too wide to fit through the door to the stage. The kids weren't too rattled, but their coach had that odd sheen about him of a patient slipping into shock. A painful miscalculation with an important life lesson: Measure twice, cut once.

A Ticking Clock

Another team spent six minutes of its eight-minute limit arranging props onstage. Its skit was barely under way when the clock ran out. Heartbreaking for the kids, but with another important life lesson: Balance perfection against time constraints.

During another skit that was rapidly unraveling on stage, a mother in the audience began weeping openly. Tears of pride? Tears of anguish? Who can tell at these things?

We judges had been braced for pushy parents—"Little League syndrome," one veteran called it. Most of the big people behaved, though for some of them it was all they could do to not leap onstage and deliver their children's lines for them.

As the day progressed, a clear trend emerged: The first-year teams were being trampled by the more experienced squads that had refined their judge-wooing abilities over several years. It proved the competition's main point—that creative problem-solving can be taught.

But the most valuable lesson for my money was that hard work pays off.

By nightfall, we had our winners, and the kids celebrated by pouring onto the gymnasium floor to dance to very loud music. Good news, adults: Thirteen-year-olds are just as spastic today as they were back in 1973.

As they hopped and bopped, they gave me a creative idea of my own: If only I could harness all their runaway energy, I wouldn't pay another utility bill for the rest of my life.

Turning the Tables on Telemarketers

Well, it's nice to know I'm not alone.

When I unveiled my guerrilla Telemarketer Defense Strategy in this space a week ago, I thought I was fighting a one-man battle against the forces of dinner-hour darkness.

It turns out I'm a rank amateur compared with some of you. From the phone calls and e-mails I received, I've gotta say, I'm impressed.

You guys are vicious!

Forget defensive tactics. When it comes to repelling telemarketers, most of you are firing strictly offensive weapons worthy of a Hans Blix visit. A sampling from the trenches:

"When someone asks, 'How are you this evening?' they're opening up the door, and I run with it," said Fran Johnson from Cheltenham. "I take as much time as I can to tell them exactly how I am. As a high school teacher, I have a lot to complain about. Then I say, 'Thanks for calling; I feel so much better,' and hang up."

The secret, Johnson stressed, is to never pause to take a breath.

John Cameron, a former Philadelphian now living in Australia, is on the same page: "Telemarketers always ask, 'How are you?' So I tell them, starting out with something like, 'Well, the rash on my scrotum is particularly itchy this evening.'"

Twenty Questions

Barbara Kaiser, a nurse in Philadelphia, said the inquisition defense is a winner. "When my husband answers and they ask to speak to Mr. Kaiser, he replies by asking, 'Who is calling? Where are you from? How did you get this number? What do they pay you to do this kind of work?' and so on. They get so frustrated that they hang up on him," she wrote.

Jim Stoner of Hatfield turns the tables: "Mine is, 'I'm sorry, you caught me at a bad time. But give me your home phone number and I'll call you back so I can return the favor.' They hang up. It works every time."

Charlie Maier of Philadelphia ratchets it up a few degrees.

"If it's a man who calls, the first thing I do is ask him for money. If it's a woman, the first words out of my mouth are, 'What are you wearing? What do you look like?' I don't say anything dirty, but I tell them I just like to know what the person I'm talking to looks like. It kind of puts them on the defensive," he said. "Most of the time, they will hang up on me."

All right, Charlie, you're creeping me out here. But I guess that's the point.

In his defense, he added: "I'm a person who has nothing else to do with my time, and to me the telemarketers are a great source of fun."

"My favorite Telemarketing Defense System is really an offense," wrote Sal Alioto of Rehoboth Beach, Delaware. "It goes something like this: 'Boy, am I glad you called. I just got laid off from my job. Where do I apply for a job with the company you are working for? Can I use you for a reference?' They have no choice but to answer you or to just hang up."

Cruel and Unusual Tactics

Patrick Cannon, seventy-four, a retired Philadelphia police detective now living in Warminster, shared this tip: "I say, 'I'm ninety-two years old, and I only get it [sex] twice a year. And you just interrupted!' Then I hang up."

An e-mailer from Narberth who goes by Stickman added this tactic: "I say, 'Hold on a second, there's someone at the front door; I'll be right back.' Then I just put the phone on the kitchen table and forget about them. My longest hold time was eight minutes. I get tremendous pleasure out of driving them nuts. Even better, that's eight minutes they can't call you."

And from Cheryl Branson of Boulder, Colorado: "My favorite strategy for dealing with calls for credit cards is to say, "Oh, wow! A credit card would be great! We haven't been able to charge anything since the bank took away our last one. How much will I be able to spend?' Stay on the line to hear the telemarketer try to backpedal."

"I pretend to be deaf and keep asking them to speak louder and louder," wrote Florence Hamill of Philadelphia. "That really gets them off fast."

Finally, Colen Mundy of Swarthmore baffles the phone slammers with this beauty: "I simply say, 'Sorry, but we don't have a phone at this location.'"

So, telemarketers, beware. We're armed and dangerous. Step away from the phones with your arms up.

Taking a Shot at Buying a Gun

"I want to buy a shotgun," I said.

The young man at the Wal-Mart sporting-goods counter didn't miss a beat. "What did you have in mind?" he asked, unlocking the gun case.

His name was Bob and he sported bleached hair and baggy, low-slung pants. I asked to see the cheapest shotgun he had. Bob pulled out a single-shot, 20-gauge New England brand with a price tag of $85.

Such a deal. I had come prepared to spend a few hundred.

Bob placed it in my hands. I didn't try to hide my ignorance. "How do you load this thing?" I asked.

He showed me how to break open the barrel, slide in a shell, click it shut. "Then you're set to go," Bob said.

I had come to this Wal-Mart near Quakertown, in Upper Bucks County, as a customer to see just how easy—and fast—it was to buy a weapon.

What brought me here was the suicide of Richard Lee of Willow Grove.

On February 2, police say, Lee, twenty-five, walked into a Wal-Mart in Horsham and, after passing an instant background check, bought a 20-gauge shotgun. He then drove to a Wal-Mart in Warminster, where he bought shells.

From there, he drove directly to Cavalier Telephone in Warminster, which had laid him off, and began firing. The final round, police say, was for himself.

Blessedly, no one was present for the Sunday night rampage, and Lee was the only casualty. But it doesn't take much imagination to picture what could have been had he arrived during work hours.

No Hard Questions

And so on Friday I went to Wal-Mart to experience firsthand the safeguards that failed to save Richard Lee from himself. I sighted briefly down the barrel, then said, "OK, I'll take it." I had been at the counter for four minutes.

I was waiting for Bob to grill me about my inexperience and motives for wanting a cheap gun. Had I completed a gun-safety course? Did I have any practice handling firearms?

Instead he asked me for two pieces of identification and gave me a federal form that asked a series of yes/no questions intended to root out the unstable and criminally inclined.

Had I ever been convicted of a felony? Ever been the subject of a restraining order? Any history of domestic abuse?
Mental illness? Drunken driving? Drug addiction?

If I had evil intent, did they really expect me to answer
truthfully?

I handed Bob $2 for the background check and he phoned
in my information to the state police's Pennsylvania Instant
Check database.

Ten minutes later, he returned with a box and packed my
shotgun into it.

"Does this mean I passed?" I asked.

"Yep. No problem," Bob said.

I asked if I could buy shells for the shotgun, too. Bob apologized and said store policy did not allow that.

We wouldn't want people to start shooting until they were
safely out of the store now, would we? If the ammunition re-
striction was meant as a deterrent, it wasn't much of one.
There was a Kmart across the street that sold ammunition.

On Second Thought

Bob rang up my sale, and I reached for my credit card. Once I
paid, I was free to walk out with my new weapon.

But I didn't really want this weapon, and at Wal-Mart, as
with other gun shops I checked, all gun sales are final. No returns; no exchanges.

And so at the last second, with apologies to Bob for wasting
his time, I pulled the plug on my little experiment and walked
out of the store empty-handed. The entire process had taken
twenty-seven minutes.

Just for kicks, I drove across Route 309, walked into Kmart,
and bought a box of twenty-five Winchester Super-X game-
load shells for $3.79. No ID required; no questions asked.

On the way home, I wasn't feeling particularly homicidal or suicidal or deranged. But had I been—and had I not aborted my shotgun sale at the last moment—I would have been, in Bob's words, "set to go."

I later checked with the state police in Harrisburg, who confirmed that Bob had properly done everything the law asks of him. Pennsylvania requires no gun-safety training. No proof of competence. No cooling-off period. Not even an overnight delay. Just twenty-seven minutes and two forms of ID.

That wasn't enough to stop Richard Lee. And it won't be enough to stop the next Richard Lee, either.

Lush Oasis Acts as a Winter Tonic .

The snow was falling steadily Wednesday morning as I slogged my way through Schwenksville in Montgomery County. Route 29 was a slush pit. Salt streaked my windshield.

The temperature: Twenty-two degrees under leaden skies.

At that moment I would have signed over the kids' college funds to be transported far, far away to a sun-drenched tropical island. That's when I spotted the big glass conservatory emerging from the gloom.

It stood fifty feet high, a Victorian-style steel framework covered with hundreds of glass panes. It looked as if it belonged in London's Kew Gardens, not out here where the closest landmark of note was Graterford prison.

Ott's Exotic Plants, the sign said. Hmmm. I pulled over, hopped through the slush, and opened the front door. Right away I knew I'd come to the right place.

A blast of muggy air hit me, so rich with raw oxygen I felt I was on a ventilator—only better, because this oxygen was perfumed with gardenia and orange blossom. Palm trees and figs towered to the top of the glass dome. Giant ferns spilled onto the rock paths, and plump goldfish swam lazily in the pond. A bougainvillea, its purple blooms glowing like neon, vined up the panes toward the sky.

I could almost feel my winter-dry skin sucking in the moisture.

Drinks, Anyone?

The place was empty, as quiet as a convent. Perfect. Now if I could just get my hands on a lounge chair and a piña colada, I'd be all set—the cheapest tropical vacation in history.

From the back, a man appeared in jeans and a corduroy work shirt. Owner Godfrey Ott.

As it's a slow time of year (the poinsettia rush is over, and Easter lilies are still a couple months out), he had time to talk. And so we stood surrounded by orchids, gingers, and banana plants as Ott, who is sixty-two but looks a decade younger, told me the story of this botanical oddity in the middle of a farm field.

It all began in 1914, when Ott's grandparents migrated from Germany and bought a small farm here. His grandfather farmed, and his grandmother grew vegetable plants in glass frames to sell to gardeners.

Her business flourished with the help of her young son, who—despite paralysis in both legs—hauled plants by horse and wagon to Norristown, where he sold them door-to-door.

That crippled boy—he spent his entire life on crutches—grew up to take over the nursery business, and to father several children, including Godfrey Ott, the man I stood talking to.

The business grew. Greenhouses went up. And forty-odd years ago, Ott's father began to build his dream botanical conservatory and fill it with a jungle of tropical plants.

A Labor of Love

The place, it is clear from looking around, is part tourist attraction but mostly labor of love. Many of the plants are not even for sale.

"He worked like nuts," Ott said. "Never took one day off in his life—literally, not even Christmas."

When the father and sons were excavating for a new greenhouse, they got the idea of piling the soil into a mountain and covering it with chrysanthemums. "My dad said it would be something for the people to look at," Ott said. And he was right.

The Otts' tropical retreat became a destination. "We'd get hundreds of cars," he said. "There was nothing else to do back then."

These days, most visitors are regulars. The business' allure as a tourist draw is largely behind it, Ott agrees.

And that is half the charm. In an age of chain restaurants, formulaic movies, and cookie-cutter box stores, this stone-and-glass relic from another age, handcrafted with pride by enterprising immigrants, is a tonic, a reminder of how things once were and will never be again.

Ott plans to spend the rest of his life right here, and then he doesn't know what will happen. He has ten children by two marriages, but not one has followed him into the business.

I wish him luck and mean it. Then, pausing to inhale one last gulp of the blossom-scented, oxygen-charged air, I push open the door and step out into the slush—for the moment, at least, a renewed man.

Ditch the Speedo, and Other Florida Tips

Look! Up in the sky! What's that blotting out the sun? Is it a plane? Is it a blimp? Is it a flock of jumbo-sized Canada geese?

No, it's just the annual migration of the Great Northern Pale-Bellied Snowbirds as they flock from their home range in the Philadelphia region to the fabled winter thawing grounds of South Florida. Caw! Caw! Caw!

With the temperatures in the Northeast dancing into the single digits, the southward stream of half-frozen pale-bellies has reached a frenzied pace.

The signs are everywhere: darkened houses, boarded pets, piled-up mail, empty offices. Have you tried to find long-term parking at the airport lately?

The featherless snowbirds are heading south en masse, some for a few days, some till spring, and I only have one question: Will the last one out please leave me his long johns?

Unlike most migratory birds, the Great Northern Pale-Bellied Snowbird is not protected under federal law, which makes sense, I guess, considering it's the only known avian to fly coach class wearing loud clothing.

I spent twelve years living at ground zero of the annual invasion—Palm Beach County—observing the pale-bellies interact, often disastrously, with the native species. I want to help.

Here's the first thing snowbirds need to know before taking flight: Floridians will smile as they take your money, but make no mistake, they're laughing at you behind your back. Snowbird character assassination is a favorite pastime in the Sunshine State—and there's no bag limit.

The second thing snowbirds need to know is that, balmy skies and white sand aside, it's a jungle down there. This is a place where the T-shirts read: "Don't shoot; I live here!"

So I've put together these Snowbird Survival Tips to help my migratory neighbors avoid harm and ridicule while thawing out:

Leave the Speedo at home. I know it looked buff on you back when you were training with Mark Spitz, but time marches on. Snowbirds tend to follow the inverse rule: the larger the body, the smaller the suit. Buck the trend and cover up.

Try not to fry. Too many snowbirds assume the vacation is a bomb unless they return home sporting third-degree sunburn. The lobster look is a sure giveaway you're a Great Northern fly-in. Floridians spend years perfecting their skin cancer; don't try to catch up in a week.

Steer clear of seniors. South Florida's large elderly population looks harmless enough, but don't be fooled. I've witnessed seniors duke it out over parking spaces. In November, a seventy-four-year-old man died from a head injury after he was slugged during a scuffle in line for movie tickets. The suspect: a sixty-eight-year-old.

Don't become roadkill. Along those same lines, my advice is to stay off the roads. You think Philly drivers are out of control? We're a bunch of Mario Andrettis compared to Florida drivers, many of whom haven't had a vision test since Grover Cleveland was president. I've seen drivers plow their cars into swimming pools, store windows, fire hydrants, you name it. Mr. Magoo lives—and he drives a Buick in Delray Beach.

Speak like a local. Boca Raton, where I used to live, is pretty high on itself (probably because it has more face-lifts per capita than any other place on earth). Pronounce the town wrong, and you are marked for life. So repeat after me: Boca Ruh-TONE. Not ruh-tahhn. Not ruh-tan. Ruh-tone. If you really want to impress the locals, simply say, "Bowh-ka!"

Drop the fib. Don't call your long-lost relation in Fort Lauderdale and say, "I've really missed you, Cuz." He'll see right through it. All Floridians have had this scam pulled on them. If you want to show your Florida kin you love them, visit in August. If you want a free place to stay in February, try the homeless shelter.

Don't get lured by the early bird. That great Florida institution, the early-bird special, offers really bad food at ungodly hours for unbelievably low prices. The locals avoid these joints like typhoid. If you want to blend in, you should, too.

Now go have fun in the sun.

As for me, I'll be ice fishing.

Deaf Girl Provides Lesson in Courage

Caitlin Reel was just six months old when her mother knew something was wrong.

The baby did not respond to voices or sounds, not even a loud clap of the hands. The doctors told Luann Reel not to worry. Her baby was fine.

But the mother persisted, and when doctors finally tested Caitlin's hearing a year later, they confirmed her fears.

Caitlin was living in a world of silence. She was profoundly deaf.

Flash forward ten years to last week at Shady Grove Elementary School in Ambler. The gymnasium was filled for the winter concert.

Music teacher Ryan Dankanich stepped to the microphone and told the audience they were about to hear "a very special violinist." The only clue he gave that this student had made a particularly arduous journey here was when he said, "Make sure you applaud very loudly."

And then out walked Caitlin, now eleven, the deaf baby who never learned to give up. She lifted her violin to her chin, and took a deep breath.

In the audience, Luann, the proud mom, stood poised with a video camera. Her hands were shaking.

"I was really worried," she said later from the family's home in Parkside in Delaware County. "She had crossed a lot of barriers to get here. I didn't want something really unpleasant to come out of her violin."

A long, hard battle

What a long road it had been. From birth, her daughter had been misunderstood, stared at, whispered about, incorrectly labeled—even by a teacher—as mentally retarded.

Caitlin set out to prove them wrong. She learned sign language and the rudiments of speech. She received a cochlear implant, which allows her to hear some sound. A major accomplishment came last fall when she ordered a Big Mac and fries all on her own.

While her hearing brother, Jared, nine, walks two blocks to school, Caitlin must ride forty-five minutes or more each way. The Penn Delco School District buses her to Shady

Grove Elementary, which has a program for hearing-impaired students run by the Montgomery County Intermediate Unit.

Caitlin saw hearing students arriving with musical instruments and said she wanted to play, too. And so, despite all odds, she began violin lessons—the first deaf child at the school to attempt them.

"It's taken a tremendous amount of concentration and perseverance on her part to get to this point," said Melanie Stefanatos, Caitlin's hearing-support teacher.

And last week's concert was her chance to show the world.

The audience hushed. Caitlin drew the bow across the strings. And out came . . . music. Slow, sweet, and steady—and with rock-solid timing. She played "Mary Had a Little Lamb" and "Twinkle, Twinkle Little Star."

Her mother fought back tears.

"I know she's not playing Tchaikovsky," Luann Reel, who is divorced, said. "But this is my deaf daughter—and she's playing the violin."

An Incredible Feat

For most children, the brief performance would be just one of many Kodak moments on the road to adulthood. For Caitlin, it was a Herculean leap. To play this handful of notes, she had to overcome more obstacles than most of us will face in a lifetime.

As Dankanich, the music teacher, put it: "It's just an incredible feat she's been able to accomplish."

Caitlin probably will not go on to become a famous musician. She doesn't need to. The violin already has taught her about courage and perseverance and faith.

A girl without hearing tackled an instrument that has everything to do with hearing, and she didn't give up. For the determined, she learned, even the steepest mountains can be scaled, one step at a time.

Her performance over, Caitlin hurried off the stage. Principal Beth Pearson told the five-hundred-member audience the truth about Caitlin—that she was one of the school's seven deaf children.

The audience roared its approval—loudly enough, in fact, that Caitlin could hear the clapping through her cochlear implant.

Backstage she signed to her mother: "I'm so happy. They were clapping for me. They were clapping for me."

A Mother: Don't Turn Boy into Man

Phyllis Regan is eighty-two now and frail as a sparrow. On this day, I sit across the bed from her in her room at Regina Nursing Home in Norristown, discussing a crime she has followed closely in the newspapers.

Our subject is Dennis Gumbs, fifteen, who stands accused of throwing a large chunk of ice off an overpass near Allentown, killing a Berks County mother of three.

Gumbs remains jailed in Lehigh County's adult prison, charged as an adult with criminal homicide.

Regan thinks this is terribly wrong.

"He's being treated as an adult," she says. "But he's just a boy."

When I went looking for guidance on how society should treat a child accused of taking a life, I could have turned to legal scholars or psychologists or social workers. Instead, I decided to ask a mother.

Regan, a native of Wales who still speaks with a clipped accent, knows something about boys.

She reared three sons in Northeast Philadelphia during the turbulent 1960s. She then watched her sons raise sons of their own—two who are now out of college and a third finishing college, all with bright futures.

The six boys in her life, their photographs surrounding her now, emerged unscathed through the tumultuous roller coaster of adolescence. But she knows it could easily have turned out otherwise. "I was strict with my boys," she says. "But sometimes boys just don't think."

Acts and Consequences

There were fistfights, pranks, and bad judgment calls, any one of which could have brought tragedy. As a mother, she did her best, then said a prayer and held her breath.

Her boys made it. Many others did not. She knows this firsthand, too.

Regan asks me to open her bed-stand drawer. Inside, I find a photograph of her as a young woman. She is strikingly beautiful and wearing the uniform of the Royal Air Force.

She served as a nurse in the RAF through World War II, attending to the wounded and dying—young men, boys really, who had charged brashly off to war with no thought to the horrors that awaited them. She sees the faces of those shattered soldiers when she thinks of the boy behind bars.

"He did a terrible thing, but, knowing the way boys are, I don't think he did it with the intent of killing somebody," she says. "I'm sure he didn't. Boys act very impulsively."

Without thought to consequences.

Regan speaks on the assumption that the boy committed the act for which he has been charged. A trial will determine that.

But she cannot fathom charging a boy as an adult for a crime that has all the markings of adolescent bad judgment. In our outrage over this senseless crime, it would be easy to write off this elderly woman as out of touch. Yet she raises a legitimate question.

The Right Justice

If throwing ice off a bridge is not a juvenile crime, then what is? As tragic as its consequences were, doesn't this case belong in juvenile court? While awaiting trial, shouldn't a fifteen-year-old suspect be held in juvenile detention?

This is not the Washington sniper.

"My heart aches for the family of the mother who was lost," she says. "But just imagine the mother of this boy, too, what she must be feeling."

One life has already been senselessly lost. Should we, she asks, throw away yet another?

Regan concedes that the family of Elaine Cowell, the thirty-three-year-old mother who was killed when the ice chunk slammed through the windshield of her minivan on Route 22, "would think I'm very cruel to be talking this way." But through the prism of eighty-two years, she can see both sides of this tragedy.

"I know it won't bring the mother back," she says. "But this boy has to live with this for the rest of his life."

Will locking him up with adult inmates do anything but create another simmering sociopath?

A woman is dead, I say. Surely, we cannot simply slap the killer's wrist and send him home.

The person who did this must be punished, Regan agrees. But the suspect is a boy, not a man. He should be tried as one, she says. And, if found guilty, punished as one, too.

❦

A Caretaker for Every Dirty Need

It's a beautiful morning—freezing rain turning to slush under-
foot—as I begin my first official tour of the Main Line. My
guide for the day is a woman who calls herself Miss Poop.

What better way to get to know the neighborhood, I figure,
than with someone who has the real dirt—the one who picks
up the dog droppings.

Our first stop is an elegant house on a wooded hill overlooking Valley Forge National Historical Park. It has a four-car
garage and enough square footage to hold the entire Mummers
Parade. Miss Poop swings open the gate. The backyard is a
mess. The culprits: four large dogs, including a pair of horse-
size Great Danes.

Armed with a steel rake, dustpan-like scoop, and plastic
shopping bags ("Target's are my favorite"), she patrols the lot
in a meticulous grid pattern, leaving no turd unturned.

Without warning, the owner—an executive in bedroom
slippers—lets out the four dogs, which jump all over Miss
Poop in the mud. Obviously, you need to really love dogs to
do this job. Fifteen minutes later, she has five bags filled and
neatly knotted.

Miss Poop, also known as Miriam Hughes, a fifty-one-year-
old college graduate and trained medical illustrator from Valley
Forge, is an entrepreneur. She saw a need—well-heeled subur-
banites who love dogs but hate cleaning up after them. And so
a year ago, she launched her service under the motto, "You
deliver, we pick up!"

Ultimate Indulgence

Neither rain nor sleet nor snow can stop the Main Line's poop lady, as I found out on our recent soggy morning together as we sloshed from Wayne to Villanova to Devon, creating duty-free zones as we went.

For $15 a week, she, like a handful of other pooper-scooper services around Greater Philadelphia, takes the dirty work out of pet ownership.

Call it the ultimate indulgence for the pampered class. For a price, every unpleasantness can be farmed out to an eager member of the service economy. There are people to clean our sinks, wash our socks, clip our toenails, diaper our babies, cater our parties. And now, to even follow Fido around, shovel in hand.

Is this a great country or what?

Miss Poop insists that some of her clients are average folks just like her, but on this morning, the homes we visit are in their own stratosphere.

The second house we stop at opens directly onto the grounds of the national park. This one's a cakewalk. The two dogs that live here "only ever go in one spot," Miss Poop explains as she makes quick work of the job.

In Villanova, we stop at a large Tudor with tennis courts, formal gardens, and a Mercedes-Benz and Range Rover in the driveway. In Devon, the patio looks over a man-made lake. At each estate, the dogs have free rein.

Man, if my two middle-class mutts catch wind of this, they're going to form a union and go on strike.

One, two, three, four . . .

We're tired of sleeping on the floor!

Staying Safe Out There

As for Miss Poop, she counts her blessings in simpler ways. "There's nothing worse than having a bag with a hole in the bottom," she says.

Many of the homes she services have teenagers in them, and she says, "Sometimes I wonder why people don't have their kids doing this."

Don't hold your breath, Miss Poop.

After each stop, she sterilizes her hands and tools. The risk of disease is an occupational hazard, she says. Last summer she contracted pleurisy from, according to her doctors, breathing in airborne bacteria.

When Hughes started this business, the reaction from family and friends was subdued. "A lot of them were almost embarrassed for me. Some would say, 'How can you lower yourself?'" she says. "But I'm not lowering myself. I'm starting up a business."

She has twenty-five clients and is adding more each week. Her goal is to get big enough to support herself entirely on, well, her wealthy clients' weekly doos.

She dreams of someday having a staff of pooper-scoopers who can fan out across the region, keeping suburban backyards safe for barefoot croquet. But, no matter how successful the business gets, she says, "I think I'll always keep my hands in it."

Uh, Miss Poop? Maybe we should rephrase that.